Coca and Cocaine

Recent Titles in
Contributions in Criminology and Penology

COCA AND COCAINE

An Andean Perspective

Edited by
Felipe E. Mac Gregor (El Magico)

Translated by JONATHAN CAVANAGH
and ROSEMARY UNDERHAY

Foreword by GIUSEPPE DI GENNARO

Published under the auspices of the
Asociación Peruana de Estudios e
Investigación para la Paz

Contributions in Criminology and Penology, Number 37
James Inciardi, *Series Editor*

GREENWOOD PRESS
Westport, Connecticut • London

Library of Congress Cataloging-in-Publication Data

Coca and cocaine : an Andean perspective / edited by Felipe E. Mac
   Gregor ; translated by Jonathan Cavanagh and Rosemary Underhay ;
   foreword by Giuseppe di Gennaro.
        p. cm.—(Contributions in criminology and penology, ISSN
   0732–4464 ; no. 37)
      Translations from Spanish.
      "Published under the auspices of the Asociación Peruana de
   Estudios e Investigacion para la Paz."
      Includes bibliographical references and index.
      ISBN 0–313–28530–6 (alk. paper)
      1. Drug traffic—Bolivia. 2. Drug traffic—Colombia. 3. Drug
   traffic—Peru. 4. Cocaine industry—Bolivia. 5. Cocaine industry—
   Colombia. 6. Cocaine industry—Peru. 7. Coca—Economic aspects—
   Bolivia. 8. Coca—Economic aspects—Peru. I. Mac Gregor, Felipe
   E. II. Asociación Peruana de Estudios e Investigacion para la
   Paz. III. Series.
   HV5840.B6C6   1993
   363.4′5′098—dc20   92–12282

British Library Cataloguing in Publication Data is available.

Library of Congress Catalog Card Number: 92–12282
ISBN: 0–313–28530–6
ISSN: 0732–4464

First published in 1993

Greenwood Press, 88 Post Road West, Westport, CT 06881
An imprint of Greenwood Publishing Group, Inc.

Printed in the United States of America

The paper used in this book complies with the
Permanent Paper Standard issued by the National
Information Standards Organization (Z39.48–1984).

10 9 8 7 6 5 4 3 2 1

Contents

Foreword

Numerous studies have been made of the problems associated with the growing of coca in the Andean countries and with the use made of its derivatives. From the beginnings of modern history, coinciding with the conquest of the New World, people have debated the rights and wrongs of chewing coca and how far this ancient tradition should be respected. In the past fifteen years, coca cultivation has become a major problem due to the alarming rise in illicit demand for cocaine in the industrialized nations. Huge vested economic interests accompany this high level of demand for cocaine and cause enormous distortions throughout economic, social, and political activity in the Andean countries. The issue today is not if but how the problem can be solved without generating worse problems.

Whatever and whoever causes the problem, it remains a socioeconomic and political reality, which can neither be denied nor simplistically condemned. Governments and public opinion in general in the Andean countries support the principles enshrined in international conventions held under United Nations auspices and approved by the vast majority of the international community; both the governments and public maintain that the narcotics trade has turned a traditional use of coca into a worldwide scourge sapping human energy, fueling organized crime, and disrupting national institutions. Coca trade should therefore be combatted as effectively as possible and, given its international dimension, will require generous contributions from interested countries.

Such a vast struggle must be properly organized around an intelligent strategy, or victims of the drug trade could easily be mistaken for delinquents and be sacrificed instead of those really responsible. It is vital to bear in mind all the opposing interests and to devise a way to free society from this scourge without committing injustice in the process.

The role of the United Nations (UN) is crucial in this respect because of the international nature of the organization. The UN program (as laid down in the regulations of the Declaration of the International Conference on Drug Abuse and Illicit Trafficking and the Comprehensive Multidisciplinary Outline of Future Activities Relevant to the Problems of Drug Abuse and Illicit Trafficking, as well as in the United Nations Convention against Illicit Traffic in Narcotic Drugs and Psychotropic Substances, all approved in 1988) aims to curb supply and demand and calls for generous international aid for a fairer distribution of wealth to enable less-favored nations to compete. The United Nations views this twofold strategy as the only one capable of dealing a real blow to organized crime by attacking the two phenomena that sustain it. Nevertheless, when putting strategy into effect the distinctions between the Andean countries must be acknowledged.

This book, the joint effort of experts from Bolivia, Colombia, and Peru, inspired by the desire to help humanity free itself from drug addiction and the criminality that fuels it, is a praiseworthy, valuable, and substantial contribution toward action programs.

Giuseppe di Gennaro
Executive Director
United Nations Fund for Drug Abuse Control (UNFDAC)

Preface

An anti-drug campaign implies the existence, within civil society or in governments, of organized or dispersed resistance toward the eradication of the whole set of social phenomena known collectively as drug trafficking.

In August 1989, researchers from the Andean countries meeting in Bogotá pointed to drug trafficking as one of five causes of violence in the region; some people exercised the drug trade's multifaceted powers, others backed them, while others opposed them. Meanwhile the majority of the population had to put up with corrupt institutions and grave economic distortions.

The Peruvian Peace Research and Studies Association (APEP) has discovered signs of such resistance. APEP has undertaken the task of investigating empirically whether resistance exists and can be proved and, if so, what forms it takes and how it can be tackled. This book is the first in a series of studies planned, and APEP would like to thank the Bolivian and Colombian researchers who, with their Peruvian colleagues, took part in this study.

The United Nations also provided assistance for the work. On behalf of APEP, thanks go to Peruvian ambassador Javier Pérez de Cuéllar, former Secretary General of the United Nations, and to Dr. Giuseppe di Gennaro, Director of the United Nations Fund for Drug Abuse Control, for their invaluable help.

F. E. Mac Gregor, S.J.
APEP's President

1

The Coca-Cocaine Phenomenon in Bolivia

Even in a brief summary of the coca-cocaine issue, it is possible to provide a well-researched overview of coca-cocaine in present-day Bolivia. This chapter's analysis covers eight major topics:

1. coca—its use and areas of production, and the special nature of the soils in which it grows;
2. cocaine—the various concepts used and the statistics on the sale of it;
3. the impact of coca-cocaine on the Bolivian economy and on different institutions in Bolivia;
4. the social impact on the same economy and institutions;
5. legislation, especially laws concerning coca, and in particular Law 1008;
6. the international dimensions of coca-cocaine, the various approaches and their consequences for international relations (special attention is paid to Bolivia here and to its relations with the United States);
7. the various coca-reduction programs imposed on Bolivia and their negative repercussions, a review that includes geopolitical observations and an analysis of the Three-Year Plan for coca-reduction, drawn up under U.S. pressure;
8. a set of suggestions for tackling the problem and finding realistic ways to solve it in La Paz, Bolivia.

COCA AND ITS GROWING AREAS

Coca has been grown in Bolivia since time immemorial, its traditional use always a part of Andean culture. During colonial times, coca was used to pay the slaves in the mines. From then on, its commercial value displaced its traditional ritual usage; however, some of the ritual uses survive today among the indigenous population of Bolivia, even though weakened and modified by cultural domination.

Interdiction also dates back to colonial times, when Roman Catholic priests felt coca impeded the spreading of the gospel. Religious concern gave way to scientific considerations. Until a few years ago, it was commonly believed that coca caused chronic malnutrition among the indigenous population. Anthropological studies and laboratory tests over the past two decades, however, reveal that this belief arises from a value judgment regarding Indians and their culture.

Coca consumption appears to have followed mining output, even in the Republican period. It is also clear that the death rate of the Indians in the mines led to falling coca consumption in the first years after the Spanish conquest. Conversely, improvements in the miners' wages appear to correlate with an increase in *acullico* (coca chewing). During the Great Depression of the 1930s, coca leaf sales dropped dramatically and caused a severe crisis in the coca-producing areas of La Paz and Cochabamba. The Bolivian government decreed coca a staple (*artículo de primera necesidad*) on 4 August 1940, and ordered the sale of it in all mining camps and railway stations.[1] Midcentury, the main coca-growing area in Bolivia was the Yungas of La Paz, where it was almost the only crop. According to the 1937 and 1938 surveys, the Yungas produced 97 percent of Bolivian coca. By 1949, this figure had dropped to 89 percent.

The 1953 land reform replaced the big estates in Bolivia with small farms and the owner-worker system. The few remaining landowners in Yungas found labor scarce. Coca output plummeted and the farms were eventually abandoned. The fall in coca consumption after the land reforms is often attributed to better living standards for the peasant farmer; however, the real cause appears to have been the drop in supply after the land ownership changes.

The Movimiento Nacionalista Revolucionario (Revolutionary Nationalist Movement) government encouraged colonies in the Bolivian jungle, and new coca crops appeared, especially in the Chapare. Seasonal laborers were contracted for planting and harvesting, even though coca-growing remained very much a family affair. It is generally thought that a single family can only farm one hectare, but in Yungas, Chapare, and the northwest of Santa Cruz, they have far more area. Hired labor became common in the coca areas, altering a fundamental feature of the traditional peasant economy of subsistence farming and only small-scale exchange. Coca fosters commerce wherever it is grown and changes the relations of production. Coca is profitable compared with other crops. While investment per hectare for coca (US$800–

US$1000) is higher than for coffee or citrus fruits, and while coca needs at least three times more work as corn, rice, or bananas, it is still the choice of peasant farmers in the Yungas and Chapare. In 1972, the profits from coca-growing in the Yungas were estimated at 207 percent, and in Chapare at 332 percent.[2] The big money, however, is made by the people who market coca (*rescatadores*), particularly when they sell to the people who make cocaine sulphate.

There are three coca-growing areas in Bolivia: the Yungas of La Paz, the Chapare in Cochabamba, and the Yapacani in Santa Cruz. According to the National Department for Agrarian Reconversion (Direccion Nacional de Reconversion Agricola—DIRECO), the total area planted with coca in Bolivia in 1988 was 60,956 hectares distributed as follows: 51,198 in Cochabamba; 8,913 in La Paz; and 845 in Santa Cruz.

The Yungas is in the department of La Paz, on the eastern slopes of the Andes. It is a temperate dry forest zone, between 300 and 2,500 meters above sea level that covers 11,000 square kilometers, and its population in 1987 was estimated as 152,000.[3] The population density—13.8 inhabitants per square kilometer—is more than double the national average (6.1 inhabitants per square kilometer). The area has two provinces: North Yungas, with 21 districts (*cantones*) and 380 communities and a capital, Coroico; and South Yungas, with 20 districts of 291 communities and a capital called Chulumani. The terrain is rugged, making road building and mechanized agriculture tricky. A few subtropical rain forests exist in the Coroico, Chulumani, Covendo, Tipuani, and Apolo areas. This whole area is crisscrossed by tributaries of the Beni river.

According to the Proyecto Agroyungas study, the land in the Yungas generally has a very thin layer of arable soil and a mixture of vegetable loam and shale. Although it is easy to plough, it is sloping and easily erodible. Yields are generally low and the topsoil quickly deteriorates. The high runoff completes the destruction due to nappe erosion. Pastures are difficult to establish because they compete with wood and grass and because the soil is trampled by large animals.

There are historical references to migrations by Aymara Indians from the *Altiplano* (high Andes) to areas where they could plant coca and citrus fruits. During the colonial period, and in the first hundred years of the republic, there was a gradual population rise, but both official and spontaneous migrations have increased sharply since midcentury. The population has quadrupled over the past thirty-seven years, and the population of North and South Yungas is increasing at an annual average rate of 4.53 percent. This migration is clearly connected to coca growing, but other crops play a major role in the agricultural diversification programs in the area. Yungas produces 95 percent of Bolivia's coffee and a third of its citrus fruit. Roughly 70 percent of Yungas coffee is for export. New cultivation and soil conservation techniques have been introduced over the past decade to improve the output of citrus fruits and coffee.

To plant coca, farmers look for soils exhausted by other crops (*k'allpas*) or the lower scrublands. Land shortage (70 percent of all farms are single plots and 55 percent have under 5 hectares) and the need to make the most of *poromas* (fertile land cleared for other crops) are what dictates where coca is planted. *K'allpas*, especially if they are on the steep slopes, are only fit for growing coca. Normally coca is planted on terraces, or *huachos*. Building them can involve digging to a depth of 80 centimeters (a process known as *cavada*) and shaping the moved earth. The coca terraces may also be constructed by cutting into slopes (*zanjeo*). In these cases, the plant tends to last less long and yield less.[4] Lately, the slope system has been used increasingly (even on the fertile land cleared for other crops) to expand coca planting, reduce costs, and to meet the huge increase in demand for coca by the international cocaine trade. Hence, it is easy to distinguish new from traditional coca plots by noting how and where the terraces are built, which could help to distinguish better between a "traditional coca-growing area" and "traditional plantings" in the proper sense. Both legislation and state programs to reduce coca crops in Bolivia ignore this distinction.

Tropical Chapare is an extensive area in Cochabamba that is formed by parts of the provinces of Chapare, Carrasco, and Arani. It runs east of and parallel to the eastern slopes of the Andes. Chapare has low hills and alluvial plains. The former are alluvial formations running east of the Andes, while the alluvial plains slope slightly down toward the edge of the Amazon jungle. The great rivers of Chapare (Secure, Ichilo, Chapare, and Isiboro) rise in the Andes and flow into the Mamore, a tributary of the River Beni. On the plains, the rivers form extensive bends with wide banks. Floods occur during the rainy season. Indeed, Chapare has one of the highest rainfalls on the planet.[5] Thus, Chapare's alluvial soils have mainly formed recently. Vegetation is dense, of a kind found both in the high and low jungle. According to Flores and Blanes, "the nature of the soils in Chapare imposes severe restrictions on agriculture, due to erosion, excessive humidity, and rapid decline in fertility. Only 10 percent of soils can be used with relatively few restrictions for agriculture; 34 percent has to be used for specific crops; while the remaining 56 percent is only useful for forestry, cattle raising, or tourism." Chapare soils have little organic matter (1 to 3 percent); high acidity (4.5 percent on average), and low levels of nitrogen, phosphorus, and other nutrients. Once the land has been cleared, the rains usually wash away the organic matter in the soil, with the minerals and the ash left from burning the trees. Thus rice and maize yields are halved by the second harvest. Rains also make harvesting difficult. With coca, for instance, if the leaves are not dried within three days, they go black and lose their commercial value.

The habitation of this lush part of the planet is relatively new. As recently as 1920, only Todos Santos could be called a center of some importance, and the route to Cochabamba took eight days.

In his research on coca production and population changes, Gonzalo Flores maintains that

after the Chaco war, large settlements were formed. After 1958, colonies appeared in Puerto San Francisco, to the north of Chipiriri, and areas next to the Chimore river. As a result of MNR government policy, new migrants arrived and by 1967 there were 54 colonies with a total population of 24,000. By 1976, the area had 142,000 people, almost 20 percent of the population of the department of Cochabamba. Evidently almost 70 percent of the colonist families settled in Chapare after 1970. In other words, the occupation of this area is overwhelmingly recent.

During colonization, agricultural output proceeded as follows: first, products like bananas, citrus fruits, rice, corn, and yucca; then, in small quantities, came coca, cane alcohol, and brown sugar.

The typical migrant to tropical Cochabamba is a peasant from the valleys, high plateaux, and the mountains, in search of land. The Chapare means new land and marketable crops. The migrant will live in a commercial milieu, no longer a "peasant" but a "farmer." The settler frequently uses wage labor alongside his own. Sixty-two percent of Chapare settlers moved there because they were landless. Those that did have land were not better off: half of them had one hectare or less, and most of the larger parcels were in barren zones. In Chapare, 88 percent of the settlers have a small holding between 5 and 15 hectares, and the average is a 10-hectare parcel.[6]

Traditional crops in the Chapare were coca leaves, citrus and other fruits, rice, maize, and yucca. The cycle began once the parcel was cleared. Rice was planted because it grew better on the nutrients left by the fires used to clear the land and could be swiftly harvested for sale. Next came the joint planting of maize and yucca. In the spaces between the maize stalks, coca was planted, and it grew in the shade of the yucca plant. This rotation was intended to make coca a central crop, alongside citrus and other fruits. Over the past thirteen years, the coca crop has grown enormously in Chapare, but there is no longer crop rotation. Under boom conditions, farmers preferred to substitute traditional crops with coca and accelerate the agricultural cycle in the new land, in order to reach coca production faster. Between 1976 and 1982, coca production increased 1,100 percent. Its high price triggered a rise in the price of the remaining products. The consequences will be examined later in the chapter.

Chapare coca farming techniques have differed from those in the Yungas, where the climate and topographical conditions also differ. The Chapare farmer has no use for terraces (*huachos*) and plants coca in furrows filled with a mixture of earth, manure, and ashes. The new plants are placed 30 to 45 centimeters apart, and frequently yucca is planted between the furrows. Coca shrubs take three years to reach maturity and then are harvested every three months; the leaf is dried, packed in baskets, and taken to market. There another story starts, one that has made Chapare nationally and internationally famous.

COCAINE: DEFINING TERMS

Although international law (the 1961 Single Convention) defines the coca leaf as a narcotic and the chewing of it (*acullico*) as "drug abuse," today it would be difficult or misguided to equate coca with one of its derivatives. The United Nations recognizes the traditional use of coca and rejects the idea of total eradication, maintaining that crops should supply only traditional and other legal pharmaceutical needs. Thus the coca "problem" is cocaine. From the "surplus" coca crops to the consumption of "crack" in the United States, a network of interrelated groups constitutes the so-called "drugs transnational," the handling of one of the largest trades in the history of the world economy.

Drug trafficking has a huge influence on all domestic, social, economic, and political life and does Bolivia even more damage than the international stigma of being a drug producer. New bodies for drug-abuse control and repression, economic policy decisions, migration, the realignment of the trade unions, and even political scandals are all closely linked to cocaine trafficking.

Cocaine production has three phases: first, cocaine sulphate is extracted from the coca leaves; second, the sulphate is transformed into an oxidized base; and third, the base is converted into cocaine hydrochloride or crystals. An estimated 100 kilos of coca leaves are required to obtain one kilo of dry sulphate. Three kilos of sulphate yield one kilo of oxidized base, producing some 900 to 980 grams of cocaine hydrochloride. One pound of leaves produces one gram of crystals. Newspaper reports and even some "studies" frequently confuse sulphate with oxidized base, calling them indistinctly "paste," "base," or "basic paste" (or coca paste). The raw materials used together with the coca leaves (1) to obtain the sulphate are kerosene, sulphuric acid, carbonate, and lime; (2) to transform the sulphate into oxide are sulphuric acid, sodium permanganate, and ammonia; and (3) to obtain crystal from the base are acetone, ether, and hydrochloric acid.

The World Health Organization (WHO) defines drugs as "all natural or synthetic substances associated with the development, in variable doses, of psychological or physical dependence phenomena."[7] References to drugs do not usually include alcohol, for instance. The United Nations argue that "even though alcohol is one of the oldest psychotropic substances of general use it has not been included . . . due to the fact that it differs greatly from other psychotropic substances by the way in which it is consumed and the methods used to combat alcohol misuse." This statement reinforces the conviction that today drugs are in practice defined as "any forbidden substance," which leads to the conclusion that the legality or illegality of a substance determines whether the consumer is or is not a sick person and if the person in possession of it is an offender or not.[8]

Addiction is another concept that, together with those of "consumption," "misuse," or "abuse," can mean very different things. The WHO defines addiction as

a condition of periodic or chronic intoxication, detrimental to the individual or society and caused by a repeated consumption of a drug (natural or synthetic). Its main characteristics are: (1) a compelling need to continue taking a drug and to obtain it by any means whatsoever; (2) a tendency to increase the dosage (due to the level of tolerance created); (3) a physical dependence that requires the drug to maintain individual equilibrium (otherwise withdrawal symptoms occur).[9]

In 1964 the international organizations substituted the term "addiction" for "dependence." Dependence in the case of cocaine included: (1) strong psychological dependence; (2) no elimination; (3) no tolerance and sometimes increased sensitivity toward the drug's effects; and (4) a strong tendency to continued use.

A description of the effects of addiction appears in "The United Nations and Drug Abuse Control" published by the UN Division of Narcotic Drugs in Geneva:

In the case of abuse, the stimulating effect of cocaine produces excitement and loquacity and tiredness is diminished. Cocaine can produce euphoria and a feeling of great muscular strength. This excitement period is followed by a period of depression. Consumption of high doses of cocaine produces feelings of suspicion, fear, and hallucinations, (characteristic of paranoid delusion) which can make the user capable of committing aggressive and antisocial acts. The effects of cocaine are similar to those produced by the use of amphetamines.[10]

Cocaine is sniffed as pure hydrochloride, but in the last few years consumption of cocaine sulphate and cocaine oxide mixed with tobacco has become popular. In Bolivia this product is known as *pitillo*, and in Colombia as *basuco*. It is more toxic than hydrochloride, because of its impurities and the way it is taken. "Crack," now popular in the United States, is a mixture of cocaine, sodium bicarbonate, and ammonia, stronger than the *pitillo*. One kilogram of cocaine yields 10,000 small bags of crack.

With the rise in consumption, Latin American drug traffickers, such as the powerful "Medellin Cartel," began to displace North American organizations and to compete with them even for markets inside the United States. Crack consumption affected drug trafficking within the United States, creating very serious problems for public safety. In 1984, a kilogram of cocaine in the United States was worth US$65,000. In 1988, supply and demand lowered that price by US$10,000–US$14,000. In the city of Los Angeles, the number of gang members dealing in crack is now estimated at no fewer than 70,000 young people, reminiscent of the "Cosa Nostra" during Prohibition. Present groups, however, are larger and more violent than the old "Mafia." The Jamaican network, for instance, is made up of some 5,000 youngsters in gangs responsible for 800 killings, 350 of which took place in 1987. This kind of drug trafficking would seem an even graver social problem than consumption itself.

The term "trafficking" covers activities from coca leaf cultivation to the consumption of crack. The number of middlemen is one explanation for the incredible amount of value added in the final product, but the key factor is the illegal nature of the whole trade. Rosa del Olmo has noted that drug trafficking enterprises work like any other modern business but are considered illegal only when they create a market in the developed countries. Drugs are considered a serious problem because there is a developed market for them in Europe and in the United States. It seems, however, that the main economic benefits accrue to distributors rather than producers.[11]

COCAINE'S IMPACT ON THE NATIONAL ECONOMY

It is said that Bolivia "lives" off cocaine. An American Congressional committee recently indicated that Bolivia's yearly "income" from cocaine exports amounted to US$900 million. The conclusion is that the country "receives" two "cocadollars" for every dollar earned by legal exports, but statements like this do not explain how the "cocadollars" enter the country, who "receives" them, or how these figures are estimated. Serious estimates of the impact of the coca-cocaine phenomenon on the Bolivian economy have been made: (1) by the Economic Policy Analysis Unit (UDAPE) in 1985,[12] with the conclusions being published under the title "La economía informal en Bolivia" (The Informal Economy in Bolivia) by Samuel Doria in 1986; (2) in the government's Three-Year Plan Against Drug Trafficking; and (3) since 1987, in updates from the Undersecretariat for Alternative Development of the Ministry of Farming and Agricultural and Livestock Affairs (SDA-MACA).

By 1986, Bolivia had about 60,000 hectares cultivated with coca, of which roughly 35 percent was in the department of Cochabamba and 15 percent in La Paz. The amount produced in Los Yungas was 8,021 tons of coca leaf, and in Chapare 138,234 tons. With the coca production of the Yapacani region (1,352 metric tons), total national production would be 147,608 tons of dry coca leaves. An estimated 10 percent is for traditional use, the 90 percent balance being the "surplus production" used for cocaine processing.

Coca growers obtain an average yearly income of US$300 million from the sale of their crops. Surplus coca is enough to produce 1,200 tons of sulphate, from which 400 tons of cocaine hydrochloride could be obtained. But an investment of US$165 million is needed to transform that amount of coca leaf into sulphate; US$46 million to transform sulphate into oxidized base; and US$88 million to obtain 400 tons of cocaine hydrochloride. This means that if all the surplus cocaine is transformed into cocaine hydro-chloride, the overall investment required would be almost US$600 million, without including transport, security, bribes, and so on.

The profit margin is the difference between the above costs and prices paid for cocaine paste and hydrochloride in the local and international markets. The Undersecretariat for Alternative Development estimated that in 1987 the sale of cocaine paste had earned US$1,036 million for local drug traffickers, and that as cocaine hydrochloride sold in the international market, it might have generated approximately US$7,800 million in 1987 (considering only 313 tons). In their book *El sendero de la cocaína* (The Cocaine Path), Alain Delpirou and Alain Labrousse point out that in 1984 the price of one kilogram of cocaine hydrochloride was US$60,000 when entering the North American market.[13] That same kilogram when "cut," that is, mixed with other sub-stances, is sold in small doses to consumers for a total of US$600,000. By the same token, Bolivian cocaine must have moved some US$78,000 million in the North American market in 1987. It is clear that North American cocaine dealers make ten times more than the Bolivian producers.

As for the effects of these figures on the Bolivian economy, it is often said that the gross domestic product (GDP) of the coca-cocaine circuit is similar to, if not higher than, the GDP of the rest of the Bolivian economy, and that the value of cocaine exports exceeds that of legal exports by three to four times; however, it is difficult to know how much of this foreign currency remains within the country and how it is used. The UDAPE study assumes that only the coca leaf value remains while the value added (the amount by which the original product increases in value) in cocaine goes abroad. Capital flight, therefore, is calculated by subtracting the coca's value added from the export value of the cocaine. In 1985 the resulting figure could have been no less than US$5,732 million. Delpirou and Labrousse state "that what is left in the country is a significant amount for the formal and overall economy, even though it might represent only 15 percent of the resources generated by the sector." The US$367 million dollars that, according to UDAPE estimates, remain in the country "finance the formal and informal activities of the Bolivian economy."[14] This would explain why, in spite of the steady fall in formal sector GDP (more than 25 percent between 1980 and 1985), there are expanding activities, like smuggling, consumption of luxury goods, financial speculation, and so on.

The UDAPE study notes how the foreign exchange flow has supported exchange rate stability despite the 1985 drop in international tin prices and the 1986 fall in the price of gas. Only cocaine export money explains the stability of the exchange rate in the last five years and the increase in foreign exchange reserves during the early months of 1986. That same year, the government drew up its Three-Year Plan Against Drug Trafficking. There, for the first time, government officials recognize and estimate the magnitude of the coca-cocaine circuit. The increase in coca production contrasts with the negative annual average growth rate of formal economy GDP. Likewise, while the cultivated areas show a population growth of 366 percent from 1978 to 1986, open unemployment increased from 5.7 percent to 20 percent from 1980 to 1986, respectively. Including coca, agriculture grew by 61 percent between 1980 and 1986. If we disregard it, however, the sector only expanded by 4 percent over the same period.

The Three-Year Plan, like UDAPE, estimates gross capital flight by deducting the value of coca from that of cocaine exports, which results in between US$1,780 million and US$2,300 million for 1986. This massive supply of cheap dollars has macroeconomic consequences: the Bolivian currency is overvalued against the dollar; fewer internationally tradable goods are produced; imports and contraband, particularly of luxury items, increase; and local industry is damaged.

The UDAPE study adds that the 1986 balance of payments estimates show the significance of drug trafficking in the economy; the "errors and omissions" account shows a positive balance of US$175 million, largely attributable to activities connected with this sector. Again, the Bolivian economy traditionally requires around US$680 million total liquidity to function normally. Because of hyperinflation (more than 50 percent a month) and the large supply of "drug money," in 1986 the economy functioned with a legal total liquidity of only US$340 million, while some US$200 million more were obtained from cocaine trafficking.

The UDAPE study points out, finally, that consumption patterns, and hence the productive apparatus, are further distorted. The fact that services expand while primary and secondary sectors weaken reflects this. In 1986 the tertiary sector of the economy accounted for more than 55 percent of GDP. It was estimated that informal, unregistered commerce handled resources approaching US$350 million, which is equivalent to 80 percent of formal trade, and that smuggled goods reached an annual average of US$300 million in the last few years, which is equal to between 40 percent and 60 percent of legal imports.

The procedure proposed by UDAPE, the economist Samuel Doria, and the Three-Year Plan to determine capital flight resulting from the cocaine traffic seems less than adequate. Were this procedure applied to the most recent estimates made by the Undersecretariat for Alternative Development, the capital flight figure would be US$7,543 million for 1987, or fifteen times the total value of legal exports. This calculation of capital flight refers only to the coca grower and the international trafficker; however, in the coca-cocaine circuit, at least eleven different functions have been identified, and we may assume that in each there is a retained, as well as generated, value. Simplification of these calculations ignores informal use of profits which includes bribes, the "tax" that corrupt officials collect for turning a blind eye toward trafficking. There are capital investments in agro-industry, cattle breeding, real estate speculation, and transactions involving local banks. These investments do not use capital resulting from the sale of coca leaves but from the cocaine export trade.

In a different approach, Humberto Vacaflor[15] states that the bankruptcy of several "financial" or "business" enterprises and the continued fall in the price of coca leaves indicate that drug trafficking has diminished but "certainly not because of control campaigns against it." The cocaine trade, Vacaflor adds, is an economic phenomenon and its decline must have economic reasons. The decrease is probably due to other countries—Brazil, for instance—having moved into the cocaine market; the preference of the "lines" in the consumer centers for nearer countries; the struggles between national trafficking organizations over market location and consolidation; and the appearance of "crack," which is inexpensive and uses little cocaine.

Other researchers, such as Pablo Ramos, have tried to demonstrate how economic policy in force since 1985 attempts to attract capital generated by cocaine trafficking through free trading of dollars on the *bolsin* (small stock exchange) of the Bolivian Central Bank. Reports of the connivance of economic policy instruments (increases in bank interest rates to promote savings, the sale of foreign debt bonds, etc.) with capital derived from the drug trade have sparked debate in which legal, political, moral, and economic aspects are frequently mixed. The government maintains that these capitals receive no privileged treatment, but recognizes that they are important in activating various economic sectors.

Most recently, Carlos Toranzo Roca, author of *Bolivia, deuda externa y desarrollo* (Bolivia: Foreign Debt and Development), has related the growth of the coca-cocaine circuit to Bolivia's redefined pattern of accumulation. Toranzo says:

It is no mystery to anyone that (Bolivia) is undergoing the most severe crisis in its history: the centuries-old mining industry collapsed with the depression in the tin market. The crisis in the pattern of accumulation is evident; the decline in the industrial working class, the increase in migration to the coca production areas, conversion of a large number of coca growers into producers of cocaine paste; all these phenomena reflect a debasement of the economy.

The production of coca—basic paste—cocaine tempers the crisis. The surpluses obtained provide a breathing space while the pattern of accumulation is redefined.
. . . The coca-cocaine influence is felt in the inability of justice to repress it; in politics, where some politicians have no qualms about using this source to finance their activities. The police and Armed Forces do not remain uncontaminated by the business; dependence is reinforced by the presence of DEA (Drug Enforcement Administration) detachments, which have carte blanche in the Chapare and in other coca-growing areas, although . . . they have no success in their action against drug trafficking. This clearly undermines society and the State. These are the best arguments against payment of the foreign debt, in order to be able to combat drug trafficking via economic development and a revised pattern of accumulation capable of replacing the coca economy. Funds set aside to service the debt should be recirculated internally in order to generate the recovery and expansion of the production system which might generate employment with salaries high enough to stem the exodus into coca production.[16]

Flores and Blanes indicate that the normal practices and social patterns in the farmers' economy have changed considerably:

These changes vary from alteration of production patterns, soil use, migrations, settlement and the relations between Chapare and the rest of the department, to changes in market composition, the organization of trade circuits and the expansion of marketing and monetary activities in the area including new links between the Chapare settlers and other spheres of economy.[17]

The terms of trade in the traditional farmers' economy have also altered. Coca puts more money into farmers' hands than any other crop. In Chapare, according to Flores and Blanes, coca growing has generated a market economy to the point that "life is impossible without a permanent money income. In Chapare no family could survive outside the money economy (using barter) because all the needs imposed by Chapare require money if they are to be satisfied."[18]

Again, by pulling the prices of other products along with it, coca has also brought about an increase in land prices and speculation. However, probably the most significant impacts are that the settlers in Chapare and in the new areas of the Yungas are increasingly dependent on cocaine trafficking capital, and that the number of growers involved in processing cocaine sulphate is rising daily. This increase helps maintain the surplus coca crop, even when the sales price goes below its production cost.

Flores and Blanes conclude that the

bonanza created by drug trafficking is false because it lacks stability. . . . As long as drug traffickers can keep coca prices high, the situation of false wealth in Chapare will persist. But . . . a decrease in coca prices will hit the local village markets, fewer people will migrate to Chapare looking for work, trade will be reduced, and the now-inflated capacity of the Chapare settler will suddenly disappear.[19]

The increase of coca growing in recent years contrasts with a decrease in land used for other crops. In 1986 the total area planted in the country was 100,000 hectares less than in 1985, an 8 percent reduction in the national total. This decrease, together with a decline in productivity, reduced agricultural output in 1986 by more than 500,000 metric tons (MACA, Agricultural Statistics). Taking those figures, the US$300 million gross value of coca-leaf production represents 45 percent of the total value of Bolivia's crop and stock output, which is estimated at US$750 million.

THE SOCIAL IMPACT OF COCAINE TRAFFICKING

The contention that Bolivia "lives off" cocaine trafficking recognizes not only the influence the trafficking has on the economy but all its social and political consequences as well. Migration and population growth in the coca-growing areas, employment generation, realignment of unions, social mobility, increase in local consumption of the *pitillo* and of cocaine hydrochloride, changing attitudes to the "drug problem," and the national and international political repercussions are some of the main social and political dimensions of the coca-cocaine circuit. How many people are caught up in this circuit? To start with, the coca farms are usually described as "family businesses," each hectare supposedly supporting one family. It is said that one family could not plant more than one hectare because of the work involved and the time it takes to harvest. According to Flores and Blanes, however, in Chapare, 88 percent of settlers own a plot averaging 10 hectares, and approximately 55 percent of the settlers in Chapare hire farm laborers to keep up with the work. However, as numbers are impossible to estimate accurately we will use the ratio of one family (5 persons) per hectare.

In 1986 there were almost 60,000 hectares of coca throughout the country, which meant that 350,000 persons made their living from it. Federico Aguiló puts this figure at 300,000, and the Three-Year Plan talks of 350,000. According to the plan, in

1978 the number of families involved in coca growing was 15,000 while in 1986 it rose to 70,000 families, of which almost 85 percent were concentrated in Chapare in the department of Cochabamba and the rest in the Yungas in the department of La Paz. The figures indicate a population growth between 1978 and 1986 of 366 percent, or an annual rate of 21 percent. . . . This means that in 1986 more than 5 percent of the Bolivian population depended directly on drug trafficking (*sic*). As for the Economically Active Population, the evidence suggests that almost 6 percent depends on this sector.[20]

However, not only coca growers are involved. Aguiló affirms that since 1985 "half a million inhabitants (are) involved in the production and marketing of coca leaves, most of them farmers; that is to say 7.17 percent of Bolivia's total population. This data may be conservative in 1988."[21]

More light is shed on the problem, however, by a study of the social system that produces these conditions. The excessive division of land in the valleys and the lack of jobs in the cities are the two main causes of migration to the tropical and subtropical areas. The rise in coca growing over the last decade reflects the serious problems of the whole rural sector, not only the increase in the international demand for cocaine. It is also widely recognized that the newly settled areas do not even have rudimentary educational, health, or housing services. Since the prime economic activity in the area is illegal, the workers have no rights. Often enough wages are paid in kind (cocaine sulphate), and normally there are no social benefits.

Transforming a traditional farming economy into a strongly market-oriented economy entails major cultural changes. A system of barter and mutual support is replaced by competition and profit seeking. New consumption patterns and proximity to crime change the lives of a large portion of the rural population. Coca growers suffer a social stigma. The Three-Year Plan talks of "reincorporating coca growers into society and giving them the opportunity to rebuild their lives."[22] This language reflects not only the deprecation but also the compassion felt toward coca growers in Bolivian society. At times people admire their power to make political and trade union demands; at other times they are accused of being responsible for the drug "cancer," or scourge. Within the trade unions, coca growers represent the vanguard of a sector—the farmers—which over the last ten or fifteen years has gradually been displacing the traditional mining sector. On the other hand, their situation *inter criminis* forces them to sign an agreement with the government recognizing a "common enemy" (drug trafficking), which gives them some weight vis-à-vis national and international programs for crop reduction. This in turn makes the growers spokesmen for the "national interest" versus "imperialism." Contrary to other trade unions who equate their power with their distance from official policies, the coca growers' federations have gained power by coordinating with those policies. They have progressed from "valid" to "necessary" interlocutors, unlike other unions whose criteria and demands can be completely ignored by the government.

The recent decision of "resettled" miners to go into coca planting in view of the lack of employment alternatives and government indifference has strong political and social connotations: What is strange here is the miners' use of this decision for political negotiation and social awareness. The coca-cocaine circuit's capacity to generate employment while state companies are closing down has been acknowledged for years. The resettled miners announced they were going specifically into coca planting when crop prices offered a future worse than unemployment. Clearly they were implicitly announcing they would be processing cocaine sulphate. The Department of Coca Leaf Control hastened to grant the miners 800 new permits to commercialize coca in the Yungas.

As for domestic cocaine consumption, there is recent and evident concern about its effects on society and public health. Various surveys have been made to determine the characteristics and the prevalence of drug consumption. A review of this literature shows how difficult it is to establish the incidence of drug consumption. Practically all of these studies have been financed by international agencies interested in reducing the coca crop that justify their activities in the name of the "tremendous impact" of drug consumption on Bolivian society. One of the agencies frequently quoted in official documents states that, by 1985, 11 percent of the population between twelve and twenty-five years of age were "regular consumers," while 8 percent were "occasionals." The number of "drug addicts" was 80,000, slightly over 1 percent of the Bolivian population.

As the Caracas daily *El Nacional* wrote, "Some statistics on drug consumption must be stoned." Indeed, worldwide, except in Bolivia, "occasionals" are more numerous than "regular consumers." We have also seen how ambiguous a term like "addiction" can be. More recent research, such as that conducted by the Inter-disciplinary Center for Community Studies (CIEC), has identified some of the causes of the rise of drug consumption in Bolivia, led by social and economic privation. The Bolivian Red Cross has alerted others about the more common consumption of inhaled drugs and marijuana, substances that are not included in some studies oriented toward finding more cocaine consumers every day.

We are convinced that "misuse of drugs" is a serious social and public health problem, but we view it as one of several social, cultural, and political problems that determine the population's living standards. Preventive education and social rehabilitation programs isolate the problem and have more to do with institutional policies and the crusades "against drugs and in favor of life." The issue is perfect for the reinforcement of the accepted social behavior and the fight against "deviations." Consumption prevention policies in Bolivia often imagine a society besieged by the "scourge of drugs." In the seminars organized to see "what are we doing about the drug threat," expressions like "the plague," "pest," "cancer," "third world war," "evil," and "diabolical" are common. The communications campaigns of the type "Say no to drugs" by the Drug Education Campaign (CESE) and "There's still time" by the Anti-drug and Social Mobilization Education System (SEAMOS) have been intended to prove that the American Embassy and private enterprise, respectively, are worried about "drug addiction." But their approaches make them inefficient and even counterproductive for reducing the "demand for drugs."

LEGISLATION[23]

The findings of the 1961 U.N. Convention on Narcotics, introduced as law in Bolivia by the government of the National Revolutionary Movement and amended according to the 1972 Vienna Protocol, approved a set of norms and provisions to limit the use of narcotics to medical and scientific purposes. The list of substances subject to control includes not only cocaine (benzoilecgonine methylic ether), but also the coca leaf. In consequence, the *acullico* (traditional practice of chewing the leaves) was defined as "undue use of drugs."

As the Center for Development Information (CID) has pointed out, the 1961 Convention on Narcotics expresses this view clearly. *Illicit traffic* is described as "the cultivation or traffic of any kind of narcotic, contrary to the dispositions of this Convention," and *production* is defined as "the separation of opium, coca leaves, cannabis, and cannabis resin from the plants which produce them." Therefore to *cultivate* coca constitutes in itself a crime of *illicit trafficking* and the coca harvest becomes narcotics *production*. The Convention implicitly presented the coca growing peasant as a criminal and established that "chewing coca leaves is forbidden for 25 years from the moment this Convention comes in force" (Article 49, Section c).[24]

Although the Convention left it to each country whether to interdict crops as the best way to "protect public health," some recommendations and dispositions clearly promoted eradication: "If possible the parties will enforce the uprooting of all coca shrubs which grow in the wild and destroy all those which are grown illicitly" (Article 26). The MNR government ratified the 1961 Convention and in 1962 (10 January) approved a narcotics law that curiously omits the mention of coca leaves, but on 20 November of that same year a supreme decree ordered a census of coca plantations and banned new coca plantations. The Ministry of Agriculture began a crop substitution program.

In 1966 a government Inter-Ministerial Narcotics Commission started an exhaustive research project to (1) reduce and gradually eradicate the coca plantations by replacing them with other crops; (2) reduce coca leaf chewing, until the "harmful habit" disappeared; (3) fight the drug traffic, especially the cocaine traffic; (4) fight drug addiction in the country. In 1973, Law No. 11245 created the National Office for the Control of Dangerous Substances (DNCSP). The new legislation followed the norms of the 1961 Convention, which classified the coca shrubs and leaves as "narcotics" (Article 7). The law established the gradual registration of growers and "the gradual, systematic, and planned reduction of coca leaf cultivation in the country, by substituting it with other crops as profitable or more so" (Article 55).

In December 1974, a US$8 million pilot project financed by the United States was approved to determine the chances of a long-term program to reduce coca production in the country. This project led to further bilateral agreements signed in 1977, 1978, and 1979. In each one, the United States provided substantial financial help for the DNCSP to fight against cocaine traffic, including US$11 million for agricultural development projects in the Yungas and Chapare. Thus was born the Chapare-Yungas Development Project (PRODES), an inter-ministerial agency for crop substitution with United States Agency for International Development (USAID) technical and financial assistance. The PRODES legislation was revised in December 1976. The new decree established a Plan for Integrated Development, which would restrict cultivation to legal demand levels. Two years later, the government ordered the registration of all coca retailers and transporters. On 13 June 1979, under the government of General Padilla Arancibia, a new Law (No. 16562) was passed that excluded coca leaves from the list of narcotics, though it banned new coca plantations and the expansion of registered ones.

On 25 November 1981, the government approved Law No. 18714 to Control and Fight Dangerous Substances, which subjected the reduction of plantations "to the PRODES financial, technical, and organizational capacity to reach the legal coca producer and offer him the promotional long-term credits and the technical help needed to substitute his coca plantations for other crops of similar profitability." The law established that the National Anti-Drug Traffic Council, through the DNCSP, would "buy the coca leaves and sell them, seeking a certain profit margin to balance supply and demand, for traditional chewing, medical, and pharmaceutical purposes." "Collection sub-centers" were set up where coca growers had to sell their produce. Transport of coca except through the competent authorities was forbidden. Thus the 1981 law established the state monopoly for the sale and purchase of coca leaves, and banned all plantations outside the department of Cochabamba and La Paz.

The 1981 law revealed a deeper knowledge about coca leaf retail and crop substitution. The precept that alternative crops had to be "of similar or higher profitability" was rejected, and the benefits of integrated development were given more attention. In their comments on the 1981 law, Canelas and Canelas and Flores and Blanes agreed that the collection sub-centers never worked as intended. They gathered only a fraction of "legal" coca, and even that controlled quantity finally ended in the drug factories: in the first quarter of 1982, the Santa Cruz State coca store sold 67 percent of its inventory. The regulations of the collection sub-centers encouraged corruption and abuse, and the prices of the sub-centers were lower than those offered by cocaine traffickers. In May 1985, when Siles Zuazo was president, new Regulations for the Control of Dangerous Substances recognized all drugs regulated by the 1961 Geneva Convention on Narcotics and specified that "preparations of the coca plant and leaves" were also to be controlled.

The regulations governing coca established that "the DNCSP would define traditional coca areas in the Yungas and Chapare, taking into account traditional practices and the maximum production in each area. Plantations beyond those areas were illegal and should be destroyed." The law gave ninety days' notice for registration under the voluntary crop eradication programs. After that, "coca plots declared illegal will be cleared by force." The use of chemical defoliants was forbidden; surveillance systems for land in potential coca-growing areas were established; cultivation of coca shoots for transplanting was forbidden and crop reduction was encouraged even in the traditional areas, in order to reach "a balance between supply and demand for traditional consumption and other licit uses of the coca leaf" (Article 42). Finally, the law replaced the collection sub-centers with a system of primary, central and final markets: the coca was to be sold by the legal producer to the distributors, then to retailers, and on to traditional consumers in the final markets. All buying and selling of coca outside the markets was strictly forbidden.

On 19 July 1988, the government approved Law No. 1008 for substitution plans and control of drug trafficking. Unlike earlier laws, the Coca Regulations and Controlled Substances Law incorporated the diverse points of view expressed by the government, coca farmer organizations, political parties, members of Congress, and even the American Embassy over several months of not always peaceful negotiations. Law 1008 distinguished the coca in "a natural state which does not harm human health" from the coca *inter criminis*

used for the production of cocaine. This distinction reinforced the recognition
of a licit use of the coca leaf as a social and cultural practice of the Bolivian
people (Article 4), defined as "necessary production," while coca *inter
criminis* was "surplus production." The new legislation established three
zones of coca production in the country: (a) traditional; (b) surplus in transition; and (c) illicit. The first covered the present plantations in the provinces
of North and South Yungas, in the department of La Paz, and in the Vandiola
zone of Cochabamba. The surplus production in transition zone

is that where the planting of coca results from a process of spontaneous or organized
colonization, and where the growth of demand for illicit purposes has caused an
increase in surplus crops. This zone is subject to yearly reduction, substitution, and
development plans through the application of an Integrated Development and
Substitution Program. (Article 10)

The illicit production zone was the rest of Bolivia. Illicit plantations would
be forcibly eradicated, and the planter would receive no compensation
(Article 11). Substitution was no longer the mechanical, and utopian, act of
planting other crops in areas formerly planted with coca, but was "a means
for changing the social and economic patterns established with the proceeds
of coca leaf trafficking, so encouraging alternative and licit, social and
productive activities capable of producing enough income for the family unit
to survive" (Article 13). Evidently all those "patterns established with the
proceeds of coca leaf trafficking" affected the entire national economy, but
that logic would have led the legislators to unexplored territories of the
coca-cocaine issue.
     Law 1008 repeated the rules for coca producers, retailers, and transporters
as state regulations, not the "monopoly" previously coveted by the state. The
new Law defined terms for the Integrated Development and Substitution
Program (PIDYS). Article 21 established that "the alternative development
and the substitution of coca plantations will aim especially at benefitting the
small coca grower of the (a) and (b) zones defined in Article 8." Law 1008
contained one of the most important concepts of the agreement signed
between the government and the coca growers in June 1987, stating that "all
coca crop substitution will be done gradually and parallel to the implementation of sustained socioeconomic development plans and programs in
the previously defined (a) and (b) production zones" (Article 22). It also
stated that plans must include provision for domestic and foreign markets for
alternative crops. The new legislation determined that the state would grant
the coca growers in the (a) and (b) zones a "fair and immediate indemnity"
and would give them "the necessary financial and technical assistance within

the terms of the Integrated Development and Substitution Plan (PIDYS)" (Article 25).

We should point out that, as in other countries, Bolivian laws are not obeyed to the letter. Coca plantations have kept on expanding; the coca leaf trade has gone on fundamentally outside the legal markets; only very lowly cocaine traffickers have gone to jail, and so on. One judge claimed there was no evidence to try a group of notorious drug traffickers and closed the "Huanchaca case" by condemning to jail a trafficker killed months before and acquitting the rest of the accused.

THE DRUG TRADE AND BOLIVIA'S FOREIGN AFFAIRS

The question of drug production, trafficking, and consumption has gradually become a central and decisive issue in contemporary international affairs, especially for Latin America. The issue of drugs manifests itself on many levels in an international scene in which political and economic structures have seen several decades of rapid change, moving toward multipolarity through the expansion of links between different states.

While the present international order favors greater cooperation and understanding between states, it has not yet opened the way for the Latin American countries, and others on the fringes of the world economy or with minimal participation in it, to have a more decisive role in the international system, one that would enable them to resolve their most pressing social and economic problems. The foreign debt crisis that began early in the last decade has proved a setback for the hopes for growth and development of the Latin American economies, reducing even further their already negative growth and their level of participation.

Similarly, the establishment of the region's democracies is slow and contradictory. The Latin American democracies face serious threats and growing social demands that the state has usually not the funds to meet.

It is paradoxical that in a world where the prevailing sentiment is interdependence, growing cooperation between nations, and the avoidance of conflict, the question of drug trafficking has been addressed unilaterally, in terms of military action, while less importance has been attached to multilateral methods for tackling what is a transnational problem. Drug trafficking is an international problem and should be understood as such. By its nature it is complex, involving international bodies, individual countries, social groups within each country, coca farmers, financial groups that eventually reap the illicit profits, and even powerful drug-trafficking "Mafias." The causes of drug trafficking are many, and their influence over national and international affairs calls for more cooperative and comprehensive treatment of the problem than has so far been undertaken, treatment employing concerted, multilateral action to resolve conflicts and threats. The different national interests could thus find common cause in seeking mutual objectives. There is no doubt that inter-American relations are now far more affected by drug-trafficking control than by foreign debt, immigration, and supposed communist expansion in Central America.

Ten years ago, United States assessments of drug trafficking were mainly concerned with Mexico, Jamaica, Colombia, Peru, and Bolivia, which supplied marijuana, heroin, and cocaine for an avid and growing North American market. Today, however, the drug trade has spread to other countries in this hemisphere, operating in them and furthering drug production and the drugs market. The channels of illegal trade have diversified, plainly indicating a strengthening of the drug trade. All the countries of this hemisphere are now involved, either because they form a specific link in the long chain of the drug trade or because they are potential markets for the drug.

The Latin American countries are concerned about the potential political effects of head-on strategies for tackling drug trafficking on their domestic affairs, which need stability and consensus, as well as the impact on inter-American relations. In other words, Latin America is wondering whether these strategies imply yet again the curtailment of the sovereignty of each country and of the region as a whole in formulating its own policies, or, on the contrary, whether the strategies, first, will lead to options reached by mutual accord that acknowledge that Latin America and the United States have common interests and, second, will lead to a mature reestablishment of links in the hemisphere.

The drug question is the center of attention in the hemisphere and therefore influences political relations between Latin America and the United States. The backdrop to this issue is the traditional dominance and hegemony exercised by the United States toward Latin American countries, which has certainly made it difficult for successive United States administrations, Congress, or government agencies specializing in fighting drugs to participate in an equilateral diagnosis[25] of the problem with their Latin American counterparts.

The prevailing attitude in the United States at the beginning of the war against drugs was the countersupply strategy, which meant attacking the areas where the coca leaf was grown and the drug it produced and carried. This was a simple strategy that did not compromise North American civil rights, which would inevitably have meant heavier penalties for those involved in the demand. Apart from this priority, the United States' "strategic" approach led to an indiscriminate classification of those supplying drugs as criminals, and hence to a greater importance to military and police action in the Latin American producer countries. This approach clearly threatens conditions for the security of the region, since Latin American territories are made available to foreign military.[26]

The socioeconomic aspects of supply and its role in society have been accorded only secondary importance in the overall North American strategy, and aid is still given chiefly to the military and police. Thus, where supply is concerned, actions and words are far from consistent. The concept of supply propagated by the United States—the hegemonic center—has been distorted by the same reasoning as has the threat from Russia, and the more conservative lobbies and some government offices in the United States associate communism, terrorism, and drug trafficking. The North American consensus attempted to determine the causes of the problem beyond U.S. frontiers and to plan punitive measures abroad. Drugs have replaced international communism as the threat to the American way of life, thereby establishing a kind of continuity in North American strategic thinking about this region.

The Latin American countries[27] affected by the drug problem have tried to maintain a broader perspective and have consistently stressed that only a reduction in demand and control of the consumer market can be expected to deter production and supply. The Latin American position thus distinguishes the socioeconomic aspects from the purely criminal in the intensified farming of the coca leaf, later used to produce the alkaloid. In other words, the Latin American countries envisage a strategy that combats demand and changes the economic and productive aspects of supply.

Forced Cooperation

The absence of a wholly equitable analysis of the origin and nature of the drug phenomenon thus gave rise to an uneasy relationship with the countries in the Western hemisphere. Over the last ten years, this tension has been visible in the disagreements and friction between the United States and the Latin American countries directly involved. The outcome has been that the United States drew up unilateral antidrug policies, leaving the other states concerned no room to cooperate actively. The United States fell back on sanctions and imposing conditions to enforce objectives defined in Washington, which has made the necessary common analysis for countering the drug trade no easy matter, and, as a result, policies have been partial, biased, and inefficient.

The Latin American countries have realized that cooperation in counternarcotics is the result of partial agreements, in practice, generally obeying North American criteria and simply hides foreign imposition. The programs drawn up so far are the result of the power Washington exerts over these governments, using forced cooperation, and hence the various bilateral counternarcotics projects are not applied with any real conviction by the countries concerned. What is more, their results show that they are not winning the war against drugs either.

The search for successes which U.S. presidents could certify to Congress, to show that drug traffic control objectives were being accomplished, was the chief motive of the U.S. use of unilateral criteria and punishment in their dealings with countries with which there were contradictory relations. The U.S. Congress was where the severest sanctions against Latin America were decided. These policies simply hindered inter-American relations. Quite aside from the discrepancies in both the analysis and handling of the drug trade issue, the modest results of the anti-drug fight are a dangerous development in the politics of the hemisphere's greatest power. They reinforce a trend toward curtailing the other countries' sovereignty, thereby affecting their security and the margins of their political stability. The United States invasion of Panama and the announced blockade of Colombian waters and air space by the United States to prevent drugs leaving the country are both examples of how the United States contemplates sending its military forces to an involved country with an apparently "legitimate" argument: combatting drug trafficking.

Consequently, North American foreign policy on the drug question exercises its classic political realism when defining relations with the Latin American countries directly involved in the drug trade. Sanctions are stressed in the contents of the U.S. impositions on Latin America, found in both the 1986 Drug Abuse Law and the 1988 Omnibus Act. Both laws have been caught up in what is effectively the legacy of the cold war. The 1988 Omnibus Act does show more serious commitment to the control and reduction of demand but it is clear that the U.S. attitude toward confrontation and treatment of supply remains unchanged and, if anything, given the 1989 Bennett Plan, is moving toward a growing militarization of the anti-drug fight where production and traffic originate.

Bolivia's International Image

There is no doubt that drug trafficking takes a special place in Bolivia's foreign policy statements. Drug trafficking has been declared a threatening universal evil, and Bolivia's responsibility for it is therefore on a world scale; however, the fight against drug trafficking must be a shared task since Bolivia is only one link in the long chain of the drug trade—that of supply—which means its scope for countering and eradicating the drug has specific limits. This issue affects the image the world has of Bolivia and—more significantly—shapes its bilateral and multilateral activities abroad. Thus, Bolivian foreign policy and its priorities turn on this problem, while other pressing foreign objectives—primarily those for strengthening democracy and economic growth and development—must take second place.

The drug trade affects Bolivia's foreign policy principally through the image the international community has of the country—currently one with a bad name and deteriorated prestige. There is no doubt that during the last decade this image greatly undermined Bolivia's international prestige and its negotiating position with partners, bilateral or multilateral. This weakened image resulted from the collusion of the authorities with the drug trade during the government of García Meza.[28] It was then that a period of harsh international isolation began, the most negative consequence of which for Bolivia's international status was that it made the country vulnerable to the "justifiable" interference of countries in and beyond the region, which, in turn, had a far-reaching effect on domestic affairs.

Bolivia's dependence on foreign initiatives during this time only increased, in a way that went beyond just the short term. International isolation was an obstacle to international cooperation, and foreign attitudes toward Bolivia were confrontational and difficult.[29] As a result, the first task for Bolivia, as soon as it returned to a democratic system was to improve its international image. Although the domestic political order had changed, the drug reputation persisted abroad and may have worsened in view of the country's political and economic crisis between 1982 and 1985. Bolivia's democratic government had inherited considerable difficulties regarding the antidrug fight, since it had not won renewed international cooperation or a recognition that Bolivia could gain from a combined counternarcotics drive. Democracy had brought rhetoric but no clear changes. The Bolivian government must still prove that it is fighting the drug trade and that the responsibility for this fight is unilateral, that is, not undertaken with other state entities. The return to democracy in 1982 improved Bolivia's image abroad very little, because at the same time it was clear that Bolivia (1) was to be identified as a matter of course as one of the foremost suppliers of drugs worldwide and (2) was expected to confront the drug trade and eradicate it just when funds were limited because of the acute social and economic crisis.[30]

Relations with the United States

Occurring simultaneously with the deterioration of Bolivia's prestige and image abroad, its link with the United States changed most noticeably as a result of the drug phenomenon. The United States continued to play its traditional role of domination over Latin American countries, and, as a result, their domestic policies have largely been conditioned by factors foreign to the region. Bolivia's relations with the United States have been contradictory, having alternated between a tradition of either automatically aligning with Washington or of resisting subordination to foreign influence, an alternative that has not infrequently produced declarations of political autonomy during its contemporary history.

Relations with the United States were most critical at the time of the military government of García Meza, for it was then that the real scale of the drug syndicates' power to corrupt became clear. Never before had the country been subject to such international condemnation of government complicity with the drug trade. From then on, bilateral relations with the United States have been basically defined in terms of the drug issue, which is thus far one of the most serious consequences for Bolivian foreign policy because the solution of this problem has been made a condition for solving others on the bilateral agenda.

Bolivia's foreign policy has had to be formulated with priorities contrary to the national interest, reducing Bolivia's international negotiating capacity. The conditions applied by the United States over the last ten years because of the drug trade clearly show how international policy on the issue was chosen with reference to the potential disapproval or approval of the U.S. government, Congress, or other interested agencies. Thus self-determination with respect to the drug question was restricted not only because of economics. Bolivian governments suffered from the merit syndrome, an acquiescence to Washington's decisions that was not only not reciprocated by the United States, but that was, in fact, met with constant warnings about the inadequacy of Bolivia's efforts.

Bolivian foreign policy on drug trafficking is subject to two conditions: pressure from North America and the impossibility of reaching domestic consensus on the issue. In Bolivia, all the steps taken so far to counter the drug trade have been the undisguised result of stringent North American conditions. The application of the Hawkins Amendment during the government of Siles Zuazo meant constant threats that American economic aid would be suspended should certain targets of coca eradication not be met.[31] However sanctions applied from Washington simply made political conditions worse for reaching sustained bilateral agreements, and relations between Bolivia and the United States grew cool.

The drug trade has given Bolivian affairs an international importance, to the extent that the course of domestic social problems deriving from it is decided abroad, especially by the United States. It is almost inevitable that the drug problem will be taken up internationally because it is complex and is determined by foreign demand. For the same reasons, domestic political trouble such as the coca farmers' reactions to antidrug policies, eradication, or substitution of the coca crops have been the object of foreign monitoring and interference.

Domestic antidrug policy is so strongly conditioned from abroad that it cannot be directed according to national government politics. The Bolivian government has managed to establish only provisional agreement among the social groups directly involved in growing coca, but it has proved impossible to negotiate an agreement on any particular strategy. In this regard, foreign pressure has been decisive. The use of repression has damaged the domestic image of the organisms responsible: Mobile Rural Patrol Unit (UMOPAR) and the American Drug Enforcement Administration (DEA). Repression, which time and again has only affected the coca farmers, has made lasting agreements between the central government and the sectors concerned unlikely. The policing entities themselves (DEA and UMOPAR) have been visibly divided over who should run the work and the direction it should take.

The result has been a vicious circle, which has made Bolivia more vulnerable and has weakened Bolivian powers of international negotiation. The U.S. demand for suppression and for evidence that Bolivia is waging war on drug trafficking has hindered domestic agreement on the question. The government position vis-à-vis the United States has been weakening as the social conflict regarding the problem has grown. Thus despite the general condemnation of the drug trade, it has been impossible to reach general domestic agreement because the government has tried to comply with bilateral pacts with the United States, while the other social sectors consider these pacts to be unacceptable interference in domestic affairs that affects their economic interests.

On the whole, Bolivian-American relations over drugs have been more controversial than cooperative, and in recent years have been characterized by constant discord and a compulsory cooperation imposed by Washington's conditions. Bolivia's ability to negotiate is so reduced as to be a matter of rhetoric rather than a contribution to detailing priorities. As we have said, the United States favors attacking the drug supply using chiefly repressive means. The Bolivian government has accepted this analysis in part, but it also emphasizes economic development as a way of solving the problem of supply. Bolivia believes, however, that the real reason for the growth in drug production is the demand from the consumers' market.

U.S. insistence that Bolivia should adopt ever more drastic (repressive) measures in countering the drug trade has always gone hand-in-hand with measures that cut the La Paz government's scope for international negotiation. Although the U.S. president and Congress did not actually de-certify Bolivia in the terms of the 1986 Drug Abuse Law, in practice the deliberate delay in handing over financial aid to the Bolivian economy is another way the United States has acted in order to exact a more accommodating attitude from the Bolivian government. The continual revisions of pacts and agreements made to tackle the evil of the drug trade since democracy was established in 1982 demonstrates that these have been the product of incomplete studies of the problem and that, given their marginal success, others are made compulsorily but in the same spirit as the first ones: as part of unilateral demands and not as the conclusion of freely negotiated policies.

For Bolivia, however, United States recognition of the poor showing of its primarily repressive strategy and eradication and crop substitution programs may present a new opportunity to negotiate from a firm internal agreement among the key social sectors. Bolivia's sights are still clearly set on multilateral treatment of the drug problem, as the only way to reverse the rigid pattern of bilateral conditions and to let the less powerful countries take part in formulating policies that acknowledge the interests of each particular country.[32] Bolivian foreign policy has moved fast in this direction, although so far the response has been only verbal rather than active. A multilateral policy in general and also by regions, particularly in the Andean countries, promises to improve the conditions for tackling the drug trade, first by clearly assigning responsibilities for supply and demand, and second by recognizing the individual features of all the countries involved.

Thus the Bolivian government has begun to envision an economic and productive transformation of the supply, meaning that where there is a surplus of coca leaves there should be a high number of production projects and that police interdiction should be subordinate to the removal of the causes of the coca farmers' economic problems. In Bolivia's case, features such as the major consuming areas and key trade routes would indicate the use of fewer military plans and more development methods. Alternative development is still, in this sense, fundamental to the Bolivian position in international negotiations.

National Security

Drug trade is considered a serious threat to national security, a view that has been strongly argued in U.S. strategy to force military action and suppression on the centers of drug production. Low-intensity conflict was developed in response to the imbalance in North American hegemony—including that caused by drug trafficking—for the Latin American political systems. Military relations between Bolivia and the United States have gradually taken the form of a "war" against drugs, hence the constant "Joint Military Operations" on Bolivian territory since 1985. The theater of these war games has included the areas where coca is grown and the alkaloid is processed.[33] In 1986, Operation Blast Furnace was carried out with North American troops to destroy the cocaine factories in eastern Bolivia. This action paralyzed drug production and lowered the price of coca, but the price of the drug on the North American market remained unchanged. The main impact of these operations on Bolivia's international position has been that it invited a foreign power into national territory and deployed military forces across the country, on the strength of hypotheses of war that inevitably involved coca farmers as occasional military targets.[34]

A Latin American, particularly Bolivian, perspective of the effects on national security related to the drug question should bring two points back into the debate: a strong military approach to the drug problem would (1) alter the social balance of power that is the foundation of the hard-won democracy of the region and (2) clearly call into question the sovereignty of the states. In the first case, it is clear that allowing the armed forces to play a more active role as a concession to foreign demands would mean widening foreigners' sphere of action in a key political matter that, in Bolivia particularly, has absolutely no connection with the military and thus affect one of the pillars of contemporary Latin American democracy—the professional and subordinate role of the armed forces. As a result, civilian supremacy under the law would be weakened.[35] With respect to the second issue, the sovereignty of the state, the United States would increase its "legitimate" intervention if it had the cover of a military confrontation and regulate Bolivian dependence at will in the form of equipment and intelligence.

If the fight against the drug trade was made international, the community of nations would be extensively involved in it, but domestic policy should not be subject to general strategies that impose military or security regulations irrelevant to Bolivia. Accepting responsibility and making a commitment to fight the international drug trade does not mean accepting United States military initiatives; instead it means emphasizing development as the most effective means for the fight. If the drug trade does affect security, Bolivia should highlight its economic effects: the Bolivian economy must not depend on the proceeds from the drug trade, and any military action should not curtail the state prerogative of upholding democracy and national sovereignty.

In summary, the drug trade is both an inter-American and a Bolivian concern, and as such a realistic U.S. approach would favor bilateral negotiation. The United States, however, wrongly believes that Latin American affairs are homogeneous and it fails to acknowledge that there are different social groups whose attitudes toward the drug trade vary. It is also a proponent of military action and unilateral treatment supported by the exercise and show of power. As the situation stands, only a perspective that recognizes the nations as interdependent would work as a foundation for a genuine offensive against the drug trade, attacking both supply and demand. In this offensive, the most significant actions have certainly been the Latin American efforts to involve other nations in the fight against drugs, to establish clearly each nation's responsibilities, to expect each nation, depending on its material capacity, to contribute, and to define the specific nature of each case involved.

CROP REDUCTION PROGRAMS

With the worldwide increase in cocaine traffic, the international community put pressure on the coca-producing countries to cut back the crops and observe the dispositions and terms fixed by the 1961 United Nations Single Convention on Narcotic Drugs. By 1989, Bolivia should have limited coca production to the level required exclusively for "medical and scientific" uses and have put a stop to the "vice" of coca-chewing. But, although coca-chewing has been dying out, coca crops have multiplied to meet the growing demand of cocaine consumers, especially the demand from the developed countries, which has caused the adoption of urgent measures to reduce the supply and demand of drugs internationally.

Let us examine what applying the economic terms of "supply and demand" to the drug problems means. For many years, international organizations classified the countries involved in drugs trafficking as "producers," "in transit," or "consumers." Bolivia, for instance, was a "producer" country, because it had abundant coca crops, while the United States was a "consumer" country, because it had a large "addict" population. This classification, however, ignored problems of consumption that occurred in Bolivia and the drug production that was carried out in the United States. It was said that the producer countries were becoming consumer countries in an attempt to present the complexity of the problem without abandoning simplicity of terminology. Nowadays, the expression supply and demand is used because it reflects the transnational character of the drug trade, but the new terminology disguises the old classification: the "supply" is found in the "producer" countries, and the "demand" in the "consumer" countries.

What is the importance of these contentions? First, the terms supply, demand, producer and consumer are only employed for opium, coca, and to a lesser extent marijuana derivatives, not synthetic drugs. They are only applied in the case of "narcotics" crops in less-developed countries. Second, the terms understate the transnational nature of the traffic. For a coca farmer, the "demand" is not some remote "consumer" in Manhattan, but the owner of a small cocaine sulphates factory. Similarly, for that consumer, the "supply" is the pusher on the corner and not a forgotten campesino in the Andes. The international traffic provides the major demand and supply and plays a more decisive role in political and economic terms than the poles of farming and consumption.

The terminology has not shed light on the problem of the drug trade, but it has distinguished an international division of labor. The last few years have seen established the idea that this should be a combined effort: the "producer" countries and "consumer" countries should reduce the "supply" and "demand" proportionately. Nevertheless, the international community has preferred to attack the weakest link in the chain—the coca crops—despite the higher social cost of this action. We can see that to reduce "demand" for drugs, the "consumer" countries have attempted nothing but educational campaigns, whose results have been ineffective, if not counterproductive. The notion "combined effort" has meant nothing more than mounting crop eradication programs in the "producer" countries with aid from the "consumer" countries.

Thus, just as the drug trade was declared illegal only when markets in the developed countries opened (in the case of opium, for example), crop reduction programs are considered essential only when they are to take place in the less-developed countries. The example of marijuana is powerful proof: the reduction of cannabis crops could not be postponed when Mexico, Jamaica, and Colombia were the main producers but when it was recognized that marijuana had become one of the United States's chief crops, it was no longer generally considered a serious problem. It is also true that the terms supply and demand are part of the capitalist world market. Protectionism leads the developed countries to bar foreign products and promote their own. It is cheaper to finance a crop reduction program and collaborate with the police force of a "Third World" country than it is to mount a program to reduce drug consumption drastically in a developed country. Reductions would also mean a saving in the consumers' expenditure, while it would mean a loss of income for the growers, but the developed countries do not think twice about such considerations of sentimental insignificance. Yet who would think of using the same force on the cocaine consumers that is suggested for the coca farmers?

This international division in the "fight against drugs" leads necessarily to the political relations between the states. The U.S. government did not hesitate to send troops to Bolivia in 1986 to persecute traffickers and bring down the price of coca, but only in May 1988 after much debate did Congress decide that U.S. troops should help control the situation in their own country. Until then, military action had been restricted to the Latin American countries of Bolivia and Panama.

Nevertheless, the history of coca would never have continued without the acquiescence of Latin American governments. From 1982's Five-Year Plan for coca crop reduction and drug traffic suppression, to the 1986 Three-Year Plan for fighting drug traffic, governments tried to keep up with their internationally contracted obligations. The Five-Year Plan was a statement of intent designed to attract funds for integrated development in coca-growing areas and to suppress the cocaine traffic. In its introduction, the

Five-Year Plan indicated that "this plan recognizes the obligations of the UN Single Convention, and . . . is based on the assumption that it is more feasible to control the supply of the drug where it originates or is produced." The Three-Year Plan was based on the same supposition and was also designed to attract international financial cooperation. In both cases, the contentions of the developed countries that wanted to reduce the coca crop were accepted, but the developed countries demanded a kind of indemnity in return.

The Five-Year Plan was made public in September 1982. Two years earlier, the United States had suspended diplomatic relations with Bolivia, following the coup d'etat that brought General García Meza to power. One of the United States's conditions for renewing diplomatic relations and economic cooperation was that work should be begun on a crop reduction program. The governments of that period felt obliged to give a good showing after the "coca-dollar" coup. Canelas and Canelas have described the ups and downs of the Five-Year Plan and the struggles of the Bolivian Government's National Anti-Drug Trafficking Council to put national interest before U.S. pressure.

Nevertheless it has been evident since then that the Bolivian government has tried to meet the demands of the international community by placing a high, though insufficient, price on its crop reduction programs. Just as "aid for development" came conditioned to crop reduction agreements, these agreements were subject to "international cooperation." A document signed by government authorities and representatives of the coca farmers in May 1982 states:

In view of Bolivia's profound economic and financial crisis, the implementation and schedule of the above-mentioned Plan is conditional on the international community and the countries which want the surplus coca-crop to disappear providing prompt, sufficient and systematic cooperation. If this cooperation does not exist or is interrupted, the Five-year Plan will be inevitably delayed and even declared void.[36]

The organization in charge of carrying out crop substitution programs was the Chapare-Yungas Development Project (PRODES), assisted by USAID-Bolivia. At first it worked in Chapare, but it moved to the Valle Alto region in Cochabamba, which had a high rate of emigration and a large number of cocaine sulphate factories. The PRODES staff were aware that it was better to provide some solutions in an agricultural area that did not have coca crops but that had problems that caused increasing migration toward Chapare than to work with very dubious results in the areas where coca was already grown.

In the Yungas, the Agroyungas Project has been running since 1985 with US$20 million of Italian support channeled via the United Nations Fund for Drug Abuse Control (UNFDAC). The Agroyungas Project's exclusive objective is to "lessen the coca farmers' economic dependence on the coca leaf in the areas where it is traditional and to avoid the extension of the coca crop in the newly settled areas."[37] The project works in research, social communication, farming diversification, financing (credit), agribusiness, marketing, building and maintaining local roads, constructing community buildings, and providing primary health care.

Since the Three-Year Plan was drafted in 1986, all crop reduction programs have been run from the Integrated Development and Substitution Program (PIDYS), a subsidiary of the Ministry of Agriculture (MACA) Assistant Secretariat for Alternative Development. The application of the Three-Year Plan originally depended on the approval of the new law on controlled substances, which was debated in parliament from the same year and was passed in mid-1988. Two years earlier, at the beginning of 1986, the government had organized a forum to inform U.S. government representatives and some international bodies about an application for financial assistance to reduce the coca crops and suppress cocaine traffic. The first version of the Three-Year Plan, which had two appendices, was debated in the U.S. Congress but was never officially published in Bolivia. Only at the end of 1986 did a copy reach Bolivia's national press, followed by the publication of two appendices in February 1988. In other words, Bolivians had to learn via independent publications of the content of a plan that their government had capitulated to pressure from the U.S. government. To date, none of the documents mentioned has been officially published.

The first version of the Three-Year Plan had four more confidential sections, apart from that on interdiction:

farming development replacing coca crops; a credit fund for economic reactivation, to make funds available for other sustained productive activities; the regional development plan, for creating the infrastructure for these activities; and the prevention and rehabilitation of drug addicts to reincorporate them into society.[38]

The farming substitution program "seeks to eliminate the surplus coca crops creating the conditions for the population to farm other products." This elimination should take place in two stages: first, by voluntary replacement and, second, by forced elimination using "compulsory means." There were two requisites: (1) "the government should have sufficient funds to provide the resources the coca farmers need to change to a new style of life"; and (2) "interdiction should be effective, producing a significant fall in profits from coca production in the national market."[39]

The reference to this "new style of life" is by no means chance, and recurs throughout the Three-Year Plan. It is telling that the US$100 million destined to compensate the families who volunteered to reduce their coca crops was designated the "Family Rehabilitation Fund" and that "the sum given to the coca farmer will enable him to change his style of life and reform society." The plan wanted to redeem the coca farmer from his delinquency and offer him a place in society. The operation has provoked just criticism for lowering the coca farmer and his family to the level of a pariah. Even more surprising are the reasons for putting this indemnity at US$2000 per hectare: "It should be explained that the compensation is less than the necessary investment for replacing the coca crop which would guarantee that the peasant farmer did not farm this crop again." If the sum of US$2000 was not enough to replace the existing crop that needed a comparatively low investment, how could it cover substituting coca with another crop?

This is where the other PIDYS components come in: (1) the Regional Development Plan extends the work of the Chapare and Agroyungas Development program with a contribution of US$40 million for an "integrated development program in the regions with high local migration" and (2) the Economic Reactivation Fund worth US$150 million opened up lines of credit to offset the "considerable fall in foreign currency earnings in the national economy" produced by the "intense campaign of action against the drug trade."[40]

Finally, there are the Prevention and Social Rehabilitation Campaigns. The Three-Year Plan states "the importance of this program increases because the more interdiction intensifies, the more (drugs) will be consumed, and more will fall back on the domestic market at a lower price." If this is true, these measures would contradict the terms of the 1961 Convention, according to which the nations will prohibit the production or use of drugs "if they believe that the conditions prevailing in their country indicate this to be the most appropriate measure for protecting public health and welfare" (Article 2). Destined for these activities was the sum of US$10 million, added to the US$100 million of the Family Rehabilitation Fund and the US$40 million of the Regional Development Plan and the US$150 million of the Economic Reactivation Fund, totaled US$300 million.

The strategy of the Three-Year Plan can be reduced to two major goals: suppression of the cocaine traffic in order to make the price of the coca leaf fall below the cost of production, and restriction of legal coca crops in traditional coca areas. The first goal, called "combining interdiction with development," aims at discouraging coca farming and offering alternatives in the coca farming areas; however, although the price of coca has fallen considerably since mid-1986, coca farming is spreading, which shows that the chosen strategy was inadequate as a deterrent to coca farming and has in fact encouraged the farmers to become sulphates manufacturers.

In 1987, PIDYS responded to international pressure by starting a hasty voluntary coca crop eradication program, paying a US$2000 indemnity per hectare. That program made more sense under the Three-Year Plan, which proposed the reduction of 50,000 hectares in one year, but it was paradoxical to begin eradication when crop expansion had still not halted. Many coca farmers took advantage of the government's desperation to collect the funds promised for the Three-Year Plan by eradicating older, not highly productive, coca bushes. Others who had stopped farming coca entirely returned to Chapare in order to receive their US$2000 offered by PIDYS for each cleared hectare.[41] Toward the end of 1988, 2,517 hectares of coca were voluntarily eradicated, but since then the coca crops have increased by 6817 hectares, according to official sources. In other words, there was a net increase of at least 4,300 hectares. The PIDYS had planned to eradicate 5000 hectares of coca during 1989 and a total of 31,000 hectares by the end of 1993, but if current trends persist, by then there will be 30,000 new hectares of coca. For the rest, it is paradoxical to make an investment of US$62 million in indemnities that brings about no improvement in alternative production or the way of life of the "beneficiary" families.

It is still more significant, however, that the state is incapable of developing the areas where coca has been voluntarily eradicated. According to the agreement signed by the government and the coca farmers' unions, eradication should take place side-by-side with regional development programs. Nonobservance of official promises frequently led to the suspension of the voluntary coca eradication program, creating social tension and clashes that had tragic results (in the towns of Parotani, Villa Tunari).

In view of this experience, the PIDYS was redesigned to include the participation of the coca farmers' organizations. This coordination has produced new policy approaches that will be applied in the course of the next few years. The international community decided to support alternative development programs in Chapare and the Yungas with a significant contribution in credit and donations. International recognition of the government's and farmers' joint effort was also evident when the Bolivian foreign minister was elected as chairman of the Convention Against Illicit Traffic in Narcotics Drugs, held in Vienna in 1988, and when the MACA under-secretary of alternative development was elected chairman of the Inter-American Drug Abuse Commission (CICAD), a department of the Organization of American States (OAS).

It is still early yet for the PIDYS. Its task is not simply substituting coca crops, but substituting the coca economy, which entails establishing a broad rural development program that influences the whole of the national economy. The policy of isolating coca and treating it differently, separating it from the rest of agricultural and national problems has been shown to be mistaken. It is evident then that to be able to "diversify" farm production in the coca areas, a market for the "alternative" products would have to be guaranteed. As Jose G. Justiniano, ex-Minister of Agriculture and Stock Farming has noted, however, the dwindling home market offers few possibilities for any farm product.[42] The development that the MACA assistant secretariat wants to create condemns this effort to isolation and failure as long as government economic policy is not modified.

It is a fact that the coca growing areas are highly unsuited to arable and stock farming. Why not create "alternative development" in the richer areas, opening up more land to agriculture and building up the production of the traditional farm land again? And why not create "survival" strategies for the majority of the rural population, which is struggling with dire poverty? The difficulties involved in "substituting" crops and the national and international dimensions of cocaine trafficking have thrown up new angles for debate.

We have attempted to demonstrate that it is the classification of coca as illegal that renders it, at this stage, uncontrollable both in coca farming and in the drug trade in the developed countries. In fact, the notion that a substance can be controlled by being declared illegal is becoming increasingly relative. If the production and consumption of the hydrochloride could be made legal, the international traffic network would collapse. The "producer" countries would not have to deal with the unofficial dependency created by the traffic; coca production would settle at a level regulated by legal demand; cocaine consumers would receive a less toxic product, not adulterated as at present; countries could levy taxes on an activity that at the moment only strengthens a black-market economy; aid programs for victims of "substance abuse" would work more effectively with people whose identity and numbers were known, and so on.

Tobacco has recently been declared a "harmful drug" in the United States. Has anyone thought of demanding a reduction in tobacco farming? If the facts described here were accepted with more flexibility, less political interference, and greater common sense, perhaps we could see the way to a solution in which the remedy did not turn out to be worse than the complaint.

PROPOSALS FOR CHANGE

In Bolivia, specific measures are needed in order to halt coca crop expansion and redirect development that could be created with international cooperation. These measures encompass eight areas for change.

Agricultural Policy. A national agricultural development strategy must include the coca farmer. As this is not a matter of substituting the coca leaf but the coca economy, solutions must be found for the chief problems of the countryside, which are the underlying reasons for coca farming expansion. To date, coca has been separated from other agricultural problems, and "alternative development" has taken the form of pilot projects. Bolivia does not need "alternative development" in the coca farming areas, but development throughout the countryside, and the coca farmer must be included in the development programs.

It is also essential to open up more land to agriculture and to provide new areas for settlement. There should be planned migration, following National Population Council (CONAPO) guidelines. Since the Cochabamba area of Chapare is very difficult to farm, the surplus Chapare population should be resettled in new areas, the valley's small landholders encouraged to return to their places of origin, and roads and irrigation works built in traditional farming areas and in areas where there is to be new production.

Economic policy must also be modified. The economic model of free goods and products imports harms traditional agricultural production. National agro-industry cannot compete with contraband and food aid. The goal of security and self-sufficiency in food production must take precedence over tax regulations and may be supplemented with preferential markets abroad, not only for crops replacing coca but for other agricultural products. The domestic market must be broadened and the price of agricultural products regulated (without subsidies), thus protecting coca farmers in the country and customers in the city.

The last few years have shown that the strategy of bringing down the price of the coca leaf to below production costs has only incorporated many farmers into the cocaine traffic ring. If there are no real development alternatives for the coca farmers, the strategy chosen by the government with North American assistance will further impoverish them. While world-market cocaine prices remain high, coca farming will continue to expand. If this is the position, there can be only two options: the "war" on the drug trade as advocated by the Bennett Plan, or the legalization of cocaine. It should not be forgotten that it is coca-cocaine's illegal status that is, in the main, responsible for the form its drug trade has taken worldwide.

Research. One obstacle for institutions, academic researchers, politicians and those who take decisions is the absence of reliable information about the drug trade. Since the drug is illegal, direct information is blocked by various interests and bureaucracy. A first step, then, would be to obtain more facts in order to make better studies and to provide the information necessary to back up action.

Exchange of Information. Since the drug trade problem affects several countries, a close-knit interdependence has grown up around it. An accurate survey of each country's information must be accompanied by the quick and easy exchange of the facts, which would help to present a more comprehensive and comparative description of all the countries. Similarly, a discussion of each nation's experience of the current state of the fight against drugs will make the Andean countries' positions on the question much stronger and more systematic. One way to achieve this exchange would be to bring out an Andean periodical that deals with the coca-cocaine cycle and related topics. A magazine of this type would be an Andean forum for discussion and analysis, and for new proposals regarding the issues arising from the drug trade.

Andean Coordination. The drug trade has become the center of attention of governments and social groups whose influences affect their countries' foreign affairs. It is vital therefore to provide information and form opinion, so that these facts are recognized and a strong Andean position on drugs established. So, too, there should be a methodical debate on the question, both nationally and internationally throughout the Andean countries, that involves the general public. Not infrequently in this matter, the government political tendencies have been to make little or no response to the demands of the general public—which should therefore be more organized. An Andean Coordination Group could make regular assessments of events and submit recommendations for particular issues to their respective governments. The group could also monitor events in the fight against drugs. Coordination, communication, and comparative analysis of national experience from an independent position would support the choices suited to each country for countering the problem.

Bolivian–U.S. Public Opinion. The civil population, organized in the Andean area via the Andean Coordination Group and working in cooperation with government policy, should submit its proposals, arguments, and demands to the U.S. public. A U.S. consensus around its punitive foreign policy is based on the distorted image of Andean countries. Reversing such views is a matter not only for the U.S. government but also for others, and a matter of paramount importance for improving the position of Latin America in the near future. Decisions must be made soon.

Andean Coca Lobby. Latin American and North American relations are established without a balance of power. The disparity becomes noticeable in the political handling of issues that concern the Andean subcontinent. The United States no longer acts as a country outside the boundaries of Latin America, but as one incorporated into the region's political systems, taking part in Latin American politics as a matter of course and frequently making or breaking domestic political affairs. The clear leading role of the United States in Latin American societies, officially recognized or not, is even more evident with the drug issue. The antagonistic effect of this role and the tremendous foreign pressure on domestic affairs are clear in Bolivia. The approaches have so far taken the form of domination, resulting in policies that tended to attack supply, and also thereby suggesting that this issue, which is a bilateral concern, must in practice be resolved here in Bolivia. In other words, the coca crops must be eradicated by force. Bolivian efficiency in counternarcotics is judged according to results seen within the country and not in relation to the behavior and responsibility of foreign drug markets.

This approach is the opposite of noninterdiction approaches, but Bolivian policies toward the United States have unfortunately been merely reactive—not that the U.S. sanctions have not been loudly disputed. One of the reasons for this response is the great weakness of the Bolivian foreign service in its dealings with the United States. It is vital that Bolivia has detailed information about the U.S. political system, the interests at stake in the formulation of foreign policy, and the process of formulating decisions on international issues.

United States foreign policy is not homogeneous or standard, but the sum of rationales having, at times, contradictory goals. Many U.S. groups have international interests in the coca-cocaine issue, in the assessment of the sectors of the country involved in drug production and trafficking, and in the treatment of bilateral relations. Well-informed assessments should change Bolivian policies on the drug trade, meaning that Bolivia would no longer be simply reactive but would show more initiative in its relations with Washington. In other words, the transparent way in which the United States decides on its policies toward Latin America should oblige Bolivia to take the initiative right there, in Washington.

Bolivia's response to the harsh conditions the United States imposes should not be simply to refuse to comply thoroughly with them, that is, to refuse to eradicate the surplus coca crops and to interdict the prohibited derivatives; its response should be to work with the U.S. groups and institutions that shape policy and formulate these demands. The training of real specialists in foreign and bilateral dealings with the United States is a matter of such urgency that Bolivia can no longer afford to ignore it.

What is necessary is the creation of a solid and active Andean Coca Lobby, which could break the bounds of conventional diplomacy and, hence, also the restrictions established by the United States. Thus an organized group, well-informed on matters of Andean and Bolivian interests, could present that information to those who make the key decisions in the U.S. Congress itself and in other responsible government departments. The United States would then handle the bilateral conditions with some reserve or doubt as a result of this possible Andean Coca Lobby. Thus Bolivia could answer the overt influence of White House representatives with a corresponding project of serious discussions within the Congress. The particular needs of Bolivia and the Andean nations should be well represented in the circles where United States policy decisions are made.

Effective discussions in United States political circles are as important as the issue at stake. Because of the drug trade, Bolivia and the Andean countries are currently in the forefront of North American strategies in the region. This is an opportunity for Bolivia to play a more active part in bilateral policy-making on the issue and also to begin to be more efficient in reversing North American sanctions and conditions, using "alternative development" in the coca-cocaine problem, the pivot of United States Andean region policy.

World Opinion. The Latin American or Andean perspective should be brought to the attention of other key countries in the international community. European countries could play a significant role supporting these proposals, and Latin American vulnerability to the United States could be reduced.

Bolivian–U.S. Relations. One immediate aim must be to be informed about the scope and direction of United States activities in Bolivia and in the Andean countries especially. U.S. counter-narcotics policy for Latin America is guided by the Bennett Plan, which insists on interdiction despite explicit recognition of the importance of cocaine demand; the modest funds and repressive approach of cooperation produced a concerted response to the plan, pressing for greater emphasis on development, a key part of any genuine attack on the drug trade.

The drug war in Colombia questions the authority of the state because of the violence and military action involved and provides ample reason to "legitimize" the stress on force in the Bennett Plan. Furthermore, the domestic upheaval produced by the drug mafia weakens Colombia's national security, which highlights another reason for an Andean alliance: to avoid the drug trade becoming a real strategic threat so that the fight against it should not become exclusively military and thereby weaken the countries even more. The drug problem should not be allowed to undermine the position of the Andean countries in relation to the U.S. military proposals contained in the Bennett Plan.

NOTES

1. Juan Manuel Balcázar, *Historia de la Medicina en Bolivia* (La Paz: Editorial Juventud, 1956), p. 503.

2. William Carter and Mauricio Mamani, *Coca en Bolivia* (La Paz: Editorial Juventud, 1986), p. 104.

3. Proyecto Agroyungas, "Monografía: Región de los Yungas" (La Paz, 1987), p. 3.

4. Gonzalo Flores, "Producción de coca y procesos poblacionales." Proyecto AD/BOL/86/409 (La Paz: United Nations, 1986). Mimeo.

5. Gonzalo Flores and José Blanes, *¿Dónde va el Chapare?* (Cochabamba: Ediciones CERES, 1984), p. 16.

6. Ibid., p. 32.

7. World Health Organization (WHO), "Expert Committee on Drugs Liable to Produce Addiction." Technical Report Series No. 21, Geneva, 1950.

8. Rosa Del Olmo, *La Sociopolítica de las drogas* (Caracas: Universidad Central de Venezuela, 1974).

9. World Health Organization (WHO), "Expert Committee on Drugs Liable to Produce Addiction." Technical Report Series No. 21, Geneva, 1950.

10. UNESCO, *El mosaico de las drogas* (Ed. Correo de la UNESCO, 1982).

11. Del Olmo, *La Sociopolítica de las drogas.*

12. UDAPE, *La economía informal: Una visión macroeconómica* (1985).

13. A. Delpirou and A. Labrousse, "El Sendero de la Cocaína" (The Cocaine Path) (Barcelona: Editorial Laia, 1988), p. 57.

14. UDAPE, *La economía informal*, p. 91.

15. Humberto Vacaflor, "Se esfuman los cocadólares," in the magazine *Ud.*, 1988.

16. C. Toranzo Roca, "Bolivia, Deuda Externa y Desarrollo" (Bolivia, Foreign Debt and Development) (La Paz: Ediciones UNITAS, 1988), p. 73.

17. Flores and Blanes, *¿Dónde va el Chapare?*, p. 76.

18. Ibid., p. 82.

19. Ibid.

20. F. Aguiló, "Movilidad Espacial y Movilidad Social Generada por el Narcotráfico," in "Efectos Sociales del Narcotráfico" (La Paz: ILDIS, 1988), p. 23.

21. Ibid.

22. Government of Bolivia, op. cit., p. 8.

23. The following Bolivian legislation has been reviewed for this chapter: Ley de Estupefacientes (Narcotics Law) of 10 January 1962; Decree Law No. 11245 of 20 December 1973—Ley Nacional de Control de Sustancias Peligrosas (National Law for the Control of Dangerous Substances); Decree Law No. 14203 of 17 December 1976; Decree Law No. 16562 of 13 June 1979; Decree Law No. 18714 of 25 November 1981; Regimen Legal de Control de Sustancias Peligrosas (Legal Norms for the Control of Dangerous Substances) of May 1985, and Law No. 1008 Regimen de la Coca y Sustancias Controladas (Norms Governing Coca and Controlled Substances) of 1988.

24. Centro de Información para el Desarrollo (CID) Center of Development Information, "Lineamientos generales de una doctrina nacional frente al cultivo de coca y al tráfico ilícito y el consumo indebido de drogas" (General guidelines for a national doctrine regarding coca-growing, drug trafficking and drug misuse), La Paz, 1987. Mimeo.

25. Juan Gabriel Tokatlián, "Seguridad y drogas: Su significado en las relaciones entre Colombia y Estados Unidos." (Santiago, Chile: Comisión Sudamericana de Paz, Documento de trabajo, 1988).

26. Juan Gabriel Tokatlián, "Drogas y seguridad nacional: ¿La amenaza de la intervención?" (Santiago, Chile: Comisión Sudamericana de Paz, Documento de trabajo, 1989).

27. Raphael Francis Perl, "The U.S. Congress International Drug Policy and the Anti-Drug Abuse Act of 1988," *Journal of Interamerican Studies and World Affairs*, Special Issue, 30, nos. 2 and 3 (Summer/Fall, 1988), 19–51.

28. LAB, *Narcotráfico y política: Militarismo y mafia en Bolivia* (Madrid: IEPALA, 1982).

29. Raúl Barrios Morón, *Bolivia & Estados Unidos: Democracia, derechos humanos y narcotráfico (1980–1982)* (La Paz: FLACSO-HISBOL, 1989).

30. Virginia Bouvier, "Bolivia–Estados Unidos: Democracia, ajuste económico y narcotráfico," *Cono Sur* 5, no. 1 FLACSO, Santiago (January–March 1986), 1–4.

31. LAB, *Narcotráfico y política II: Bolivia 1982–1985* (Cochabamba, 1985).

32. Guillermo Bedregal Gutiérrez and Rudy Viszarra Pando, *La lucha boliviana contra la agresión del narcotráfico* (La Paz–Cochabamba: Los Amigos del Libro, 1989), 454–74.

33. Raúl Barrios Morón, "Factores externos y generación de violencia en el Chapare," in *Las condiciones de la violencia en Perú y Bolivia* (La Paz: ILDIS, 1990), 125–32.

34. Michael Abbot, "El ejército y la guerra contra el narcotráfico: ¿Materia política o de seguridad nacional?" *Military Review* 68, no. 9–10 (September–October 1988), 71–89.

35. Eduardo Gamarra, "U.S. Military Assistance: The Militarization of the War on Drugs, and the Prospect for the Consolidation of Democracy in Bolivia." Mimeo, s/f.

36. "Conclusions on the Coca Leaf Reduction and Substitution Plan," La Paz, 23 May 1982 (Document signed between the National Council for the Fight against Drug Trafficking and the Campesino Federations), p. 1.

37. Agroyungas Project (U.N. BOL/84/405). "Summary of Contents and Extension as of 30 November 1986." La Paz, 1986, p. 2.

38. Government of Bolivia, op. cit., p. 13.

39. Ibid.

40. Ibid., p. 16.

41. Instituto Latinoamericana de Investigaciones Sociales (ILDIS), *El cultivo de la coca y la economía campesina*, vol. 2 (La Paz: Colección Debate Agrario, 1988).

42. Cámara de Diputados de Bolivia (Chamber of Deputies), "Seminario (Debate) sobre el Proyecto de Ley de Sustancias Controladas" (La Paz, 1987).

BIBLIOGRAPHY

Abbot, Michael. "El ejército y la guerra contra el narcotráfico: ¿Materia política o de seguridad nacional?" *Military Review* 68, nos. 9–10 (September–October 1988).

Aguiló, Federico. *Movilidad social y movilidad espacial generada por el narcotráfico.* La Paz: ILDIS, 1988.

Aparicio, Octavio. *Drogas y toxicomanías.* Madrid: Editorial Nacional, 1972.

Bagley, Bruce Michael. "U.S. Foreign Policy and the War on Drugs: Analysis of a Policy Failure." *Journal of Interamerican Studies and World Affairs*, 30, nos. 2 and 3 (Summer–Fall 1988): 194–204.

———. "Tráfico de drogas y relaciones entre Estados Unidos y América Latina," in Heraldo Muñoz (comp.) *A la espera de una nueva etapa.* Anuario de Políticas Exteriores Latinoamericanas 1988–1989. Caracas: Editorial Nueva Sociedad, Prospel, 1989. 365–83.

Balcazar, Juan Manuel. *Historia de la medicina en Bolivia.* La Paz: Editorial Juventud, 1956.

Barrios Morón, Raúl. *Bolivia & Estados Unidos: Democracia, derechos humanos y narcotráfico (1980–1982).* La Paz: FLACSO-HISBOL, 1989.

———. "Factores externos y generación de violencia en el Chapare." In *Las condiciones de la violencia en Perú y Bolivia.* La Paz: ILDIS, 1990. 125, 132.

Bascopé, René. *La veta blanca.* La Paz: Ediciones Aquí, 1982.

Bedregal Gutiérrez, Guillermo, and Rudy Vizcarra Pando. *La lucha boliviana contra la agresión del narcotráfico.* La Paz–Cochabamba: Los Amigos del Libro, 1989. 454–74.

Bouvier, Virginia. "Bolivia–Estados Unidos: Democracia, ajuste económico y narcotráfico," in *Cono Sur* 5, no. 1 (January–March 1986): 1–4.

Cámara de Diputados de Bolivia. "Seminario (Debate) sobre el proyecto de ley de sustancias controladas." La Paz, 1987.

Canelas, Amado, and Juan Carlos Canelas. *Bolivia, coca y cocaína: Subdesarollo y poder político.* La Paz: Editorial Los Amigos del Libro, 1982.

Carter, William (comp.). *Ensayos científicos sobre la coca.* La Paz: Editorial Juventud, 1983.

Carter, William, and Mauricio Mamani. *Coca en Bolivia*. La Paz: Editorial Juventud, 1986.

Centro de Información para el Desarrollo (CID). "Lineamientos generales de una doctrina nacional frente al cultivo de coca y al tráfico ilícito y consumo indebido de drogas." La Paz, 1987. Mimeo.

Comision Nacional Contra el Uso Ilícito de las Drogas (CONACUID). *La cuestión de las drogas en América Latina*. Caracas: Edición de CONACUID, 1987.

Del Olmo, Rosa. *La sociopolítica de las drogas*. Caracas: Universidad Central de Venezuela, Facultad de Ciencias Económicas y Sociales, 1985.

Di Gennaro, G. *El terreno de encuentro es la cultura*. In *Il Delfino*. Rome: CEIS, 1987.

Doria Medina, S. *La economía informal en Bolivia*. La Paz: Editorial Offset Boliviana, 1986.

Duke, James A., David Aulik, and Timothy Plowman. "Valor nutritivo de la coca." In Carter, comp., *Ensayos científicos*.

Fajardo Sainz, Humberto. *La herencia de la coca*. La Paz: Editorial Universo, 1984.

Flores, Gonzalo. "Producción de coca y procesos poblacionales." Proyecto AD/BOL/86/409. La Paz: United Nations, 1986. Mimeo.

Flores, Gonzales, and José Blanes. *¿Dónde va el Chapare?* Cochabamba: Ediciones CERES, 1984.

Instituto Latinoamericano de Investigaciones Sociales (ILDIS). *Efectos sociales del narcotráfico*. La Paz, 1988.

———. *El cultivo de coca y economía campesina*, vols. 1 and 2. La Paz: Colección Debate Agrario, 1987–1988.

Martin, Richard. "El papel de la coca en la historia: Religion y medicina de los indios sudamericanos." In Carter, comp., *Ensayos científicos*.

Ministerio de Salud, Colombia. Memorias, seminarios. Bogotá, 1987. Mimeo.

Oblitas, Edgar. *Narcotráfico, jurisprudencia*. Sucre: Editorial Túpac Katari, 1982.

Olievenstein, Claude. *No hay drogados felices*. Madrid: Editorial Grijalbo, 1979.

Perl, Raphael Francis. "The U.S. Congress International Drug Policy and the Anti-Drug Abuse Act of 1988." *Journal of Inter-American Studies and World Affairs* (Special Issue) 30, nos. 2 and 3 (Summer/Fall 1989): 19–51.

Phillips, Joel, and Ronald Wynne. *Cocaine: The Mystique and the Reality*. In *Bolivia, coca, y cocaína*, Canelas and Canelas, 1982.

Plowman, Timothy. *Aspectos botánicos de la coca*. 1982.

Proyecto Agroyungas. "Monografía: Región de los Yungas." La Paz, 1987.

———. "Resumen de su contenido y alcances hasta noviembre de 1986." La Paz, 1986. Mimeo.

Santos Chichizola, J. *Las drogas en el Perú*. Lima, 1983.

Tokatlián, Juan Gabriel. "Seguridad y drogas: Su significado en las relaciones entre Colombia y Estados Unidos." Santiago, Chile: Comisión Sudamericana de Paz, 1988. Documento de trabajo.

———. "Drogas y seguridad nacional: ¿La amenaza de la intervención?" Santiago, Chile: Comisión Sudamericana de Paz, 1989. Documento de trabajo.

Toranzo Roca, Carlos. *Bolivia, deuda externa y desarrollo*. La Paz: Editorial UNITAS, 1988.

Economic Policy Analysis Unit (UDAPE). "La economía informal: Una visión macroeconómica." La Paz, 1985. Mimeo.

UNESCO. *El mosaico de las drogas*. Paris: Ed. Correo de la UNESCO, 1982.

Young, Jack. *The Drugtakers*. London: Paladin Books, 1971.

2

The Socioeconomic and Political Impact of the Drug Phenomenon in Colombia

All dialogue presupposes the recognition of differences between interested parties, but it is precisely the purpose of dialogue to reach a common end by different paths. Differences are no obstacle. On the contrary, their presence is an acknowledgment of the fact that there is a chance to develop toward something new, which those who propose a discussion are building. Such proposals are difficult to put into effect when the participants are states not individuals. Nevertheless, this dialogue has great importance: differences in lives, culture, history, or interests are almost always discussed at state level.

In the drug issue, there has been no dialogue, since only one point of view has been presented. There has been no opportunity to compare this view with other opinions, which is what enriches the understanding of any given problem. One school of thought blames the producer countries and proposes measures that stress punishment rather than understanding. The other side accuses consumer countries of being complacent about consumption. The upshot is that the issue is polarized.

Our aim is to lay the groundwork for frank, clear, and responsible dialogue. The drug network that has permeated society makes each side self-centered and blind to the views of the other side. Hence we begin with an attempt to interpret what we believe to be at the root of the crisis in U.S. society. Then we will study the impact of illegal drugs on Colombian society: their ambivalent impact on the economy, the resulting political unrest, and the concomitant increase in violence and human rights abuses, which reveal society's lack of moral values.

The drug trade is without doubt largely damaging to society, surely the starting point for any discussion of measures to be taken. Both producers and consumers are being harmed, and that harm should not be exacerbated by irrational attitudes supporting vested interests, be they economic, political, or military.

DRUGS AND THE UNITED STATES:
A COLOMBIAN IMPRESSION

The so-called "drug problem" is still treated as one of serious risk for United States national security. While some Latin American governments and regional and international organizations have pressed the United States to adopt policies to lower demand, Washington still stresses actions to suppress supply. This strategy of suppression is built on President Ronald Reagan's slogan "war on drugs."

The "war on drugs" constitutes a threat of economic sanctions for the countries that do not accept U.S. analysis and measures, thereby subordinating all the issues of bilateral relations to the question of the drug trade. Certain penalties contained in American law have even been used to punish drug traffickers, without the penalties being consistent with the laws of the supplying countries. At the same time, the United States demands that drug traffickers—mainly Latin Americans—be extradited or has them extradited by force, thus violating sovereignty to achieve its aims. Finally the United States increasingly stresses the role of the United States and Latin American armed forces in suppressing drugs. The price of which mainly falls on the shoulders of the already deteriorated economies of the so-called producer countries. According to the summit held in Bolivia on February 15, 1990, Colombia was estimated to have lost US$2 billion in the previous three years, in damage caused by attacks and suppression expenditure: Peru US$700 million and Bolivia lost US$300 million. The result of eight years (1980–1988) following the same pattern is frustrating:

1. producer and consumer countries continue to suffer from the fact that the drug trade is illegal, with violence associated with the traffic, corrupt armed forces, judges, police and officials;
2. the consumption of illegal psychoactive substances has generally increased;
3. the number of countries involved in trafficking has increased; and
4. tension has continued between the United States and Latin America with no sight of change.

In view of these negative factors, it seemed likely in Latin America that the administration of George Bush would change its policies, which have cost the United States over US$60 billion and significant loss of life.

Nevertheless, the Bush administration underwrote the analysis and the measures. The 1989 anti-drug plan (US$7.9 billion) and the 1991 plan (US$10.63 billion) still stress suppression and extend the role of the armed forces in counternarcotics. The 1991 plan increased the armed forces budget by 50 percent (US$1.2 billion), but only destined US$313 million to social programs in the big cities and rural areas. Furthermore, the invasion of Panama, justified with the capture of General Manuel Noriega to be tried in the United States for drug trafficking, cost the lives of over one thousand civilians and deepened Latin America's distrust of United States anti-drug policy. Finally, the frustrated blockade in Colombian waters in January 1990 and the military measures of interdiction accompanying the plan show that the United States is sustaining a unilateral and unproductive attitude that violates the principles of international law and the right to self-determination.

The sectors linked to the drug trade do not offer alternatives to the socioeconomic and political system. Until now these groups have fought for partial and corporate interests, mainly for avoiding extradition. Although they face social discrimination, they do not raise the standard of a new society with a place for everyone. Confronted by the United States, they do not call for new relations between Colombia and the Central American countries that are based on respect for the sovereignty of these countries. Hence they constitute a minority group, dependent on the politics of other social and political organizations. They are incapable of linking up with other sectors or of uniting for a more general concept and so become autonomous. It seems that their inability to make their own interests dominant is due (1) to the fact that they do not distinguish them from those of the ruling class, (2) to their present differences, and finally (3) to their poor education and knowledge of history.

Today there is talk of negotiations between the state and the drug traffickers. This strategy is viable, but difficulties arise with North American opposition and with those who believe such a dialogue to be "morally impossible." The Colombian authorities have opted for a modus vivendi, avoiding rather than dealing with the problem. Another attitude would jeopardize the Colombian state and government interests vis-à-vis the United States, which seems to be the main obstacle to a negotiated settlement. Meanwhile, war and negotiations continue to alternate.

MORAL CONSIDERATIONS

Cocaine consumption, traffic, and production pose problems for the welfare of humankind. Any discussion about drug trafficking in the world therefore must consider ethics. Since the problems affect all people, the ethics should be fundamental and independent of religious, political, or specific ethnic considerations. Ethical considerations must begin with a summary of the problems:

1. Human Suffering: Coca-paste smokers are compulsive addicts, usually giving up work altogether to spend all their money on their addiction. Their families suffer; the smokers steal money in their own homes to satisfy their craving. Their neighborhoods are destroyed as communities by distrust and violence. Crack and the other forms of coca-paste smoking are producing devastating effects in other countries.

2. Social Corruption: Because of the effects of consumption, the cocaine industry is seen as a social evil, but it makes great profits and has corrupted political parties and government administrations in order to maintain its profits.

3. Impunity: As protection from the law, the traffickers have put judges in a dilemma—"silver or lead": they must take a bribe or be shot dead. As a result, state justice has collapsed and in many cases has been replaced by private justice.

4. Human Rights Violations: Colombian drug traffickers kept private armies to "wipe out communism in the country." Members of the armed forces saw this as support for the chief mission of the army, and became their allies. Military corruption followed. Finally, landowners and private industrialists started forming paramilitary groups and paying hired assassins to root out subversion. In two years these groups have murdered over 160 civilians.

5. Social Violence: Gang warfare between the Medellin, Cundinamarca, and Cali drug rings unleashed terrorism in the cities. The vendettas produced street gunfights, kidnappings, and bomb attacks, which contributed to the development of the hired assassins' market—young people hired to kill.

6. Political Violence: When the Colombian state agreed to extradite drug traffickers, the latter declared war. They murdered magistrates, high-ranking members of the government, and one presidential candidate. The state responded by declaring outright war, and drug traffickers began to attack and murder the civilian population.

7. National Autonomy: The extradition of drug traffickers divided Colombians. Many considered it a violation of their sovereignty, while others thought that because impunity had become common it was impossible to try drug traffickers in Colombia. The meaning of autonomy was discussed.

8. Economic Ambiguity: The macroeconomic effect of the drug trade in Colombia has weakened institutions (the parallel financial market, the dollar black market); distorted aggregate investment (capital directed toward less productive sectors that are covers for irregular operations); ;and distorted income distribution (land and financial capital concentration) and difficulties in monetary controls and contraband. The drug trade, however, has stimulated aggregate demand and attracted new technological investment, particularly in farming; it has generated income and created jobs and was directly responsible for raising the standard of living of nearly a million Colombians, becoming one way to

escape the crushing poverty of over 40 percent of Colombians. The Colombian economy has also had an average sustained growth of 4.5 percent during the 1980s, when the drug trade reached its peak in Colombia. This contrasts with the zero- or negative-growth of almost all the Latin American countries in the same period.

The case of Colombia proves the difficulty of finding a moral solution which is both acceptable to all and able to make policies viable. The solutions proposed for the situation described are contradictory and have no real weight. They are also repressive and inadequate. First, they are contradictory because the moral argument against money produced by the drug trade is balanced by the extensive presence of the same money in commerce, industry, and finance. Political campaigns are financed with drug capital. The state itself is infiltrated on several fronts by the drug trade. And the armed forces have not taken one definite step away from their initial alliance with the drug traffickers. Second, the solutions are unable to be taken seriously because the institutions that condemn the drug trade have been found to be involved in it. People talk about drug-controlled football, drug-controlled politicians (reforms in the constitution are blocked because parliament insists on a referendum on extradition), drug-run charities (there have been cases of the drug barons giving to church appeals), drug-run police and military (because of tacit alliances against communism and for business), and so on. Third, they are repressive because as the situation worsened the state abruptly opted for total war. Private groups also work against the drug trade, like the group trying to clean up Colombian football, threatening the players and committees with death. However, to quote Cicero in his "De Oficiis," "*Arma, non diuturnus magister officii*" (Repression is not the mentor of ethics.) It is vital that Colombia define a moral answer to address the problem less superficially, but this answer has still not appeared.

THE ELEMENTS OF A SOLUTION

We can take the following principle as a point of departure for a social ethic: "The local and international community must guarantee all people the conditions necessary for their development as people. And each person has the fundamental responsibility of promoting his or her own development, which is only possible as a part of the personal development of all." This principle requires that a person can live in a community, as human development is relational. It establishes that the person can freely promote whatever he or she needs to grow—health, affection, knowledge, liberty, and so on and should responsibly be able to avoid those things that destroy his or her own growth. It follows that each community must freely promote those elements that make it a place where all can live with dignity, and the community should protect itself with the free participation of all from whatever destroys it or weakens it as a community.

From this first principle follows another: that both people and communities are responsible for the production, or appearance in their own society, of consumer goods that threaten the life of both. It follows that people in interpersonal, participatory, and democratic communities have the moral obligation to promote all that is conducive to the growth of each person in a modern society, and that all actions, economic and political activities, and ideological contentions that are counterproductive in this regard should be avoided or redefined. One example of what is counterproductive would be a drug taken to produce happiness but that ends by destroying people and communities. Measures are often taken to prevent or eradicate evils that themselves become counterproductive, and therefore not moral. Repression and military action against drugs are not moral when they identify the industry's profits and any connections with coca with a perverse world of transgressors, thus paradoxically fostering the traffic.

The growth of people is only possible in the immediate community, which, in turn, is only viable in the long term if it acts responsibly toward all that which conditions the well-being of humanity as a whole. This world responsibility must be demonstrated by attempting to solve problems such as ecological disturbances, nuclear threats, the spread of AIDS, and drug addiction. This responsibility should finally be reflected in agreements to protect, promote, and administer issues that affect the whole of humanity.[1]

In the question of an ethic for a world democracy, the nation-state bears the moral responsibility of guaranteeing a state of affairs (judicial, economic, political) that makes possible the development of free, participatory, and pluralistic communities, which then create the conditions for personal human growth in matters that concern the whole community.

From the considerations of the individual and common good, we can deduce the following:

1. If a drug does not affect a person's responsibly defined freedom and thus restrict the liberty of the other members of the community, there are no ethical reasons for destroying or eradicating it.

2. If the derivatives and combinations of this same drug destroy people and communities by creating addiction and crime (as is true of coca paste and crack), there are individual, local, national, and world responsibilities that should be exercised to protect the person and the community. But such action should avoid counterproductive consequences and should be clearly aimed at the growth of people in free communities.

3. It seems obvious that both the international and local communities, with support

from each nation, should act against destructive and addictive drugs. This is a police matter. Similarly, there should be clear controls so that drugs that do not destroy responsibly defined freedom are not used in the production and consumption of others that do. Such drugs can be used as raw material for harmful products that create a market and produce addicts for the industry.

4. Given the development of coca paste and the consumption of crack, both the local and international communities should launch a world information and education campaign about drugs, in particular cocaine, which is the basic drug, and in general about all types of narcotics.

5. For the same reason, it is the responsibility of the local communities, supported by the states and the international community to carry out medical and psychological research to establish means of preventing drug addiction, and developing a medical cure for it.

6. These ethical considerations should be involved in the responsibility for countering the persuasive propaganda of those who produce and market drugs.

7. The distinction between those things that help or hinder the growth of people in the community is what defines the general ethical direction to be taken according to the nature of the community.

8. Finally, if an ethic is to be comprehensive, it must include changing the conditions in local communities, the states, and the international community which constitute a breeding-ground for the drug trade.

Because of economic need, millions of men and women found that producing, carrying, and selling drugs offered them a way to survive, which their unequal and impoverished societies did not. Because of the weakness of the state, many communities sought support from the industry. Because of the weakness in society, many people tried to become involved in an industry that offered them a way out of poverty and from the isolation of the countryside. Because of moral poverty, people became materialistic, judging the worth of things by the amount of money they make. Because of the lack of a sense of human dignity, men and women took refuge in drugs instead of facing their great and wonderful responsibility to build a better world for all on the basis of fraternity. It is the responsibility of all of us to fill this void and to face the vast tasks ahead.

THE USE OF DRUGS IN HISTORY

Discussions about the so-called "drug problem" start mainly with an abstract concept of humans, possessing reason and free will that they are able to exercise freely in the world around them. It would seem that the demands to open up frontiers called up a magic wand that could charm away the historical features of ethnic and cultural groups, national states in formation, or the gradual mixing of races with another perspective of the world, which they kept secret in a world carried away with its technological capacity.

How did drugs appear in the modern era? Drugs are, after all, as old as human life. Prehistoric excavations in Europe discovered poppy seed where the plant could not have grown naturally. Five thousand years ago, the Aztecs took hallucinogenic mushrooms that they called "chariots of God." The Egyptians debated the remedial value of opium, eunuch fat, and toad ashes. Greek mythology contains references to Greek warriors using draughts of poppy seed on the eve of battle. Do these habits call for a moral judgment? Not at all.

The ethos behind the cultural practices of human history surprises our contemporary notions, with its coexistence of bacchic delirium and ordered society. Adverse conditions have also led to the use of drugs: when the British Hebrides were invaded, for example, the conquered people sought refuge from their despair in drugs, which led to general degeneration.

"Killer of suffering" and "woman's friend" are the names given to drinks made from opium, which around 1840 was monopolized by the British from India and which flooded Europe. In France, opium was known by more than fifty different names; in Germany, by over two hundred. Together with ether and alcohol, already controlled at that time in the Northern hemisphere, opium had become an integral part of society. Between 1839 and 1842, England provoked the Opium War with China. With the Nanking Treaty of August 1842, England forced China to open five ports to European trade. The opium trade flourished and, from 312 tons marketed in 1798, grew to 6,500 tons in 1880. In that year, opium produced over 130 million pounds sterling for England. For China, opium produced 120 million drug addicts by the end of the nineteenth century. Hence, at the beginning of the twentieth century, a number of countries were equally responsible for manipulating the use of drugs: in World War I, for example, Germany was reported to be promoting cocaine chiefly in an inhalable form. At the end of the nineteenth century in the United States, the opium market had reached the Chinese minority brought in for labor, and cocaine reached the blacks.

In 1875 in San Francisco, the first regulations against Chinese opium smokers were issued. The 1890 law reserved for Americans the right to process raw opium into opium ready for smoking. The first report on cocaine, made by the American Association of Pharmacology, states that "together with criminals and the poor, the blacks are naturally led to consume cocaine." In almost all the European countries, drugs had already appeared in the nineteenth century, were considered a health problem, and were perhaps held in contempt by those in power. But political manipulation—which even used war as an instrument, reaching its peak in the 1914 war—brought drugs into official action, where they have remained ever since.

Traditionally, prohibition has been proposed as a solution to the problem of drugs. In the seventeenth century, the Czar of Russia, Mikhail Feodorovitch, had anyone found in possession of tobacco executed. In 1650, the Sultan of the Ottoman Empire, Murad IV, decreed the death penalty for smokers. The same fate was set in Luneberg in Germany in 1691. The first prohibition laws in China were passed in 1792. The first example of sweeping prohibitionism was established by Muhammad in the seventh century and written into the Koran, which is still the code of conduct for several countries. In the West, most prohibitionist policies were based on the Protestant ethic. A particular example of this is the role played by Archbishop Brent in the Shanghai Conference on opium and drug control. And the decisive role of the Puritans and Methodists in establishing the alcohol prohibition amendment in the U.S. constitution in the eighteenth century is well known.

Hence religion provided an argument for prohibition, one expressed in moral choice: bodily health and control or the lack of it were the consequence of grace, or the condemnation of the soul resulted when drugs were used. This argument was not exclusively concerned with individual morality. In the case of societies such as the United States, the ethical and cultural foundations were Protestant and affected politics and the way of life. As a result, nonreligious proposals for the drug question—with arguments based not on one single fundamentalist belief—still find obstacles even today.

"The beginnings of North American society show a series of propositions for the development of a MONIST MOVEMENT (read anti-pluralist) which had huge support in the United States."[2] This movement involved groups from the elite and the working class and was the basis of a number of political movements: the Know Nothings, the anti-Masonic movement, and so on, which incorporated the monist model, that is, morality and a moralistic attitude were common to the various politics that they proposed. "The first example may have been the Temperance Movement which appeared early in the nineteenth century . . . the struggle against alcohol formed part of a 'Puritan Counter Reformation' intended to influence the 'ordinary man.' "[3] There is no doubt that what remains today of that morality (even the anti-state actions so popular today) draws strength—with reference to history—from contentions of this kind.

RECENT U.S. POLICY ON DRUGS

The decade of the 1970s saw a widespread economic crisis that came to a head in the great recession of late 1973 to mid-1975, and which contributed to the breakdown of the harmonious social order and expectations of indefinite progress that had been typical of the post-war years. The fall in production in the United States was estimated at US$200 billion.

President Jimmy Carter's attempt to seek a new balance of power by recognizing the emerging multipolarity ended with a break in the two party system that had existed in the United States since the end of World War II. The center of the debate was the discussion on the U.S. "national interest," and concerned the loss of power in the world. The lack of consensus in party policies and about the handling of the economy increased the attitude of pessimism, which helped to produce neoconservative policies and Ronald Reagan's 1980 victory.

As we know, the new schools of economics see the role of the state as one of the chief reasons for the crisis:

Increased "regulation" of economic activity which extended the role of the state in the economy turns the government into a gendarme which stifles the productive process ... reflected in a lower rate of technological innovation, a fall in big company administration, and the expectation of excessive state protection, which businessmen demanded in response to the narrower margins of competition of their products at home and abroad.[4]

This was also a political criticism that accused the liberal positions of fostering national decadence with their complacent attitude toward supposed national enemies. The conservatives emphasized the importance of the family, tradition, and local organization. Thus they assured "a close link between all these factors which are considered key to the recovery of the vitality of the United States, while at the same time making use of the most advanced technical media for projecting the promise of a vigorous national recovery."[5]

Finally, there was a general questioning of Carter's trilateral international strategy intended to recognize and share certain spheres of power with other Western governments. In order to move on to another strategy of U.S. leadership, meanwhile, the North-South axis fears that dominated the 1970s were replaced by the East-West axis in the 1980s.

Ronald Reagan intended to recover the old belief that international politics begin where national problems leave off. The different spheres that made up the new leadership were treated as all the same thing. The danger was not so much the crisis of consensus concerning the leaders but that this crisis might affect the system itself. Reagan had to restore the ethical and political tradition and social consensus that in the late 1940s had grown around anticommunism and strengthen belief in free enterprise, both as a national example and a system that could beat the rest of the world.

Since the Founding Fathers, the doctrine of "North America as an exception" had been understood in the sense that the United States was "a light to the nations, immune to the social evils and decadence which have afflicted all other republics in the past, a nation exempt from all the social laws of development which all nations have finally obeyed." The underlying assumption was that "the new nation would be morally superior to any which had hitherto existed and that morality would serve as the foundation of political order."[6] The realization of these tenets, according to Daniel Bell, lies in the establishment of a "complete civil society . . . perhaps the only one of its kind in political history."[7] While growth as a national society, changing politics, and mobilization for total war have been, for Bell, necessary responses to critical moments, they have also brought the role of the state to the fore. The root of current tension then is the kind of statism that encourages total war, which—if it does unite people in the face of a perilous enemy—also means that the state must mobilize the human resources and the materials of civil society.

Reagan and the "Drug Problem"

The drug crisis in the United States in the mid-1970s also saw a rise in drug consumption, the emergence of new types, and a rise in rates of crime. The situation was so critical that there was a consensus against drugs that was greater than any since the peak of anticommunism. Amid this sentiment, Reagan offered a monistic, moralizing rationale stressing that "production" was the key to everything: the answer was the crusade against drugs to be put into effect with "total war" or "zero toleration." What was at stake in the United States was the discipline of society and those pillars of the new Right: the family, tradition, and local organization.

The emphasis on suppressing supply marked a new context for U.S. and Latin American relations. Imposing diagnoses and "remedies" are the actions of a nation looking for global and definitive solutions to the drug problem and destroys the chances of common action based on respect for differences in situation. There is no room for dialogue.

First, laws create coercive mechanisms that subject all the countries implicated in drug production to the limits defined by the United States. These laws are of two kinds:

1. The first are antidrug laws like the October 1986 law that established the *certification* system for the countries cooperating in counternarcotics, which involves the threat of complete suspension of U.S. aid, a block on loans from the international banks, a refusal to give preferential treatment to exports in the terms of General Agreement on Tariffs and Trade (GATT), or increases in import tariffs. These laws contain provisos: countries like Pakistan, Turkey, or

even the Afghan guerrillas are not *decertified.* Their geopolitical role in the East-West conflict allows them special treatment. Countries like Syria, Iran, or Manuel Noriega's Panama, however, are decertified.

2. The second kind of laws involved United States pressure for its counternarcotics laws to be valid internationally and for its courts to try and sentence the drug traffickers. Used in extradition processes, these arguments have justified the violation of the sovereignty of Honduras in the case of Matta Ballesteros, of Panama in the case of Noriega, and the threats made against Colombia.

Second, the increased importance given to the drug issue in normal international relations (trade, finance, diplomacy, etc.) has caused crises, the Colombian crisis of 1987, for example. International relations are now regulated by one single principle, and the rules are made unilaterally. The importance of the drug-trade issue affects the area of economics and shatters the margin for negotiation of any relatively autonomous state.

Finally, military pressure has been exerted. In the United States, there was a heated debate about the role of the armed forces during the Reagan administration. At first the Pentagon seemed reluctant to participate in an antidrug war. The armed forces were concerned about the possibility of funds being misused and the danger that their troops would be corrupted. In 1981, when the Posse Comitatius Act came under review by Congress, military personnel were authorized to participate in law enforcement.[8] The Congressional debate of 1988 also involved this issue. In May of that year, a new military budget was approved that gave the army a wider role in antidrug activities. This tendency grew, as we will later show, with the Bush administration.

In this area, we also find the ideological influence inherent in the participation of security forces and the U.S. armed forces. The undercover operations in Nicaragua, using counternarcotics funds to help the "contras," toleration of the Afghan guerrilla rearmament with the proceeds of the heroin traffic, the attempts in the American Armies' Conference in Mar de Plata (Argentina) in 1986 to present subversion as an integral part of the drug trade, indicate an unfortunate political tendency. Similarly, the failed "Blast Furnace" operation (to destroy cocaine factories) in Bolivia in 1986, the installation of a military base in Santa Lucia in the Huallaga region of Peru, or conventional arms aid to the Colombian military are indicative of a tendency to reestablish inter-American relations in military terms.

Bush and the "Drug Problem"

North American analysts' pragmatic attitude to the strategy followed during the eight years of the Reagan administration could be summed up as follows:

- The drug problem is a tragedy that both the producer and consumer countries share. Consumption is on the increase in the so-called producer countries.
- The drug trade has such power to disrupt that the only options open to the armed forces, judges, police, politicians, and elected authorities are corruption or death.
- At least fifteen countries are now involved in cocaine production, processing, and distribution.
- Continued United States pressure, far from finding effective solutions, has further aggravated relations with Latin America and has not resolved the problem; to the contrary, this problem has worsened.

On the basis of this simple diagnosis, it was to be hoped that President George Bush would reformulate United States dealings with Latin America, seeking the cooperation of those countries.[9]

Nevertheless, in the first year of the Bush administration, four events demonstrated a tendency to maintain the same policy, or in other words, the intensification of the strategies designed under Reagan:

1. The well-publicized September 1989 antidrug plan involved US$7.9 billion. The plan was aimed at building more federal prisons, with 26,350 extra beds. The budget increased for the law enforcement agencies (US$350 million), for deterrents and for making public the fact that occasional consumption is also punishable. It was at this moment that the proposed naval blockade in Colombian waters was made public.

2. The 1991 antidrug plan, officially published on 25 January 1990, involved US$10.63 billion, which represented a 10 percent increase on the budget at the time and called for the death penalty for the drug barons. It also increased military aid to Colombia, Peru, and Bolivia from US$125 million to US$206 million. The plan approved a counternarcotics budget for U.S. armed forces of US$1.2 billion as opposed to the previous year's US$80 million, a 50 percent increase.

3. The invasion of Panama in December 1989 caused—according to unofficial figures—over one thousand civilian deaths in the country. The supposed aim of their "just cause" was the capture and trial of Noriega for offenses related to drug trafficking.

4. The naval blockade of Colombia was attempted. This unwise move deepened Latin American distrust of the U.S. role in the anti-drug fight, and hence the blockade to be carried out by the aircraft carrier *John F. Kennedy* was aborted.

The proposed blockade indicated a worrisome tendency: Bush is involving the United States army increasingly in the "anti-drug war." The Defense Secretary, Dick Cheney, has still not given up plans for a blockade. This plan is being supplemented with new measures for Latin America:

1. radar stations will be put in Colombia, Peru, and Bolivia (the dispute will be over who is in charge of the radar);
2. there will be an increase in training counternarcotics teams for jungle warfare, night operations, topography, and intelligence for the U.S. Special Operations;
3. the groups of advisors already in the three countries will be joined by two hundred green berets and soldiers;
4. Air Force AWACS (Airborne Warning and Control System) planes may patrol the cocaine traffic route;
5. the NORAD (North American Aerospace Defense) Command, near Colorado Springs, might use radar stations allocated for fast warning of Soviet attack missiles, to re-transmit intelligence information about the drug trade; and
6. interdiction operations will also be intensified on the Mexican frontier, using armed forces personnel. This was done in Fort Blill, Texas, where one hundred members of the navy and army were assigned as support for the civilian agencies that patrol the Mexican frontier.[10]

One thing is clear: The extensive expenditure involved in preparing the United States against attacks from the former Soviet Union has produced demands in Congress for cuts in military expenditure. So it is in the armed forces' interests to increase their involvement in the "drugs war."

Strategic Readjustment

The most worrying aspect in the current U.S. [Bush] administration's antidrug strategy is its intention to reformulate the global strategy increasing the North-South confrontation. In his election campaign, Bush proposed to reestablish the two-party consensus over the most potentially dangerous issues in the relations between the two hemispheres, and particularly those between the United States and Latin America. But there are also signs that this consensus involves U.S. public opinion: in September 1989 according to *Newsweek*, 53 percent polled agreed with sending troops to Colombia to fight the drug trade. In December 1989, the same action in Panama enjoyed widespread public support.

The present crisis in socialism and the defensive attitude of Russian ideology and politics have created the right conditions for a U.S. offensive that is more strategic than ideological. Some analysts have seen this occurring in the geopolitical field. The United States's "market democracy" offense is also considered to be a matter of national security. "Free democracies" are more stable and safer. Making the world democratic became the purpose, and henceforth instruments were designed to back up the offensive: political aid and the strengthening of communications became part of a nonmilitary counteroffensive aimed mainly at the East and the "Third World." Political aid, despite budget cuts made by Congress, the creation of the National Fund for Democracy (NED), and the United States Agency for International Development (USAID) have played a key role in critical moments. This is true of the NED in Panama, which gave economic and political support to the civilian opposition to Noriega.

In these terms, the antidrug war, working for democracy (understood in the Santa Fe II paper as anti-statism), and the fight against terrorism become pillars of an ideological and political reformulation of relations between the United States and the "Third World."[11] The war against drugs is also a part of the United States's strategy to make the whole world democratic.

In the United States, feelings about the antidrug fight are still pessimistic, however. The 1989 Bush plan described the city of Washington as a "test case" in the antidrug fight. The daily average of murders in the city had increased; in January 1989 there had been fifty-two violent deaths (1.7 per day), and in the first three weeks of 1990, there had been thirty-four (1.8 per day). Disputes in the city between the federal and district agencies in charge of fighting drugs have been increasing. These disputes cast doubt on the value of the "Antidrug Czar" post created by the U.S. 1988 legislation, because the absence of a coordinating body weakened the effectiveness of counter-narcotic measures. Furthermore the prisons and rehabilitation systems are overloaded. The number of offenders in Washington has tripled in the last ten years, and there are 9,300 inmates in a prison designed to hold 7000. Neither drug abuse nor violence has diminished in the United States capital.

DRUGS IN THE "THIRD WORLD"

The drug picture in the "Third World" is dramatic: plantations of *cannabis* (marijuana) are spreading in Mali, the Ivory Coast, and Senegal as a result of the collapse in peanut and cacao revenue. Ethiopia is increasing its production of *qat* (the leaves of which contain a number of alkaloids, including cathinone, which produces euphoria and its chemical structure is similar to that of amphetamines) to offset the crisis in the coffee market, the country's main source of export revenue.

Morocco is also producing marijuana, and recently coca has been found in the Philippines. In Afghanistan, Iran and Pakistan (the "Golden Crescent"), India and Nepal, nearly 1,400 tons of opium are produced each year. Five hundred tons are processed into 50 tons of heroin, of which 10 tons are exported to Europe and 3.5 tons to the United States. Lebanon produces 60 tons of opium in the Bekaa plain, and these are processed into 6 tons of heroin, which are exported to Europe (4.5 tons) and to the United States (1.5 tons). In 1988 in southeast Asia, 1,550 tons of opium were produced in the golden triangle area: Burma (1,200), Laos (300) and Thailand (50). Mexico exported 5 tons of heroin to the United States in 1988.

In some regions the production increases—above all in opium and heroin—have financed wars: the conflict in Afghanistan quadrupled heroin production over the last four years. In Lebanon there is an evident changeover from marijuana crops to opium, and in Burma the Communist Party, the armies of the Drug Lord Khun Sa, and the uprisings in the Shans states have all been financed by the revenue from drugs.[12]

This situation contrasts with the socioeconomic drama of the "Third World": a foreign debt of one billion dollars, more than one billion people in extreme poverty, and an average 30 percent fall in the price of exportable raw materials, just to mention a few general figures. We do not support the theory that there is a direct relation between poverty and the increase in drug production. It is one of the more important factors in play in the Southern Hemisphere, and it looks as if it is going to deteriorate even further since there is no visible solution to either the economic crisis or the drug problem. Nevertheless, if we are at the beginning of a new phase of the North-South axis, the drug issue will be at the top of the agenda.

DRUG TRAFFICKING IN THE COLOMBIAN ECONOMY

The export of marijuana and cocaine has led to the rapid growth of a gangster bourgeoisie that has destroyed the economic hegemony of the financial groups of the oligarchy and the more recent generations of business magnates by having obtained, in less than a decade, assets equivalent to at least 40 percent of the total wealth of Colombians. This process, with its undermining both of law and order and the pillars of political regime, has shaken the rigid political institutions that run the country and the social hierarchy. The values once embraced by national leaders have been abandoned, and most of the closed-shop bureaucratic apparatus corrupted. The forces of law and order have been infiltrated, and there is the assassination on a massive scale of the political wings of guerrilla movements and the corruption among them. The country's structures, therefore, are in disarray, which will force changes that are already apparent in public opinion regarding the reform of the state and the rules that should govern politics.

The importance of drug trafficking can be seen not only in the fact that it generates close to 4 percent of the GDP and 3 percent of employment—which is no mean feat—but also because it provides the economy with dollar liquidity. The legal balance of payments, under pressure from having to service Colombia's partly refinanced debt, has been relieved by the inflow of black-market currency, which keeps levels of saving and investment higher than they would otherwise have been. Recognizing the magnitude of the narcotics business as a whole is fundamental to getting to know Colombian society and the Colombian economy as well as the changes, at times violent, that the drug trade brings about. This recognition is fundamental also to cope with U.S. demands to eradicate the trade, in every stage of the cocaine process, which implies an economic cost that the Americans should recognize and compensate for by providing alternative legal opportunities.

The growing and export of marijuana were significant enough economically to the country in 1975 to mean that for the first time the black-market dollar was selling for less than the official price, which brought about a large surplus of dollars, soon to be expanded by the export of refined cocaine.

The estimates shown in Table 1 are obviously rough and are mainly based on the Drug Enforcement Administration's (DEA) calculations, which are, in turn, based on U.S. consumption. These estimates are derived from the coca acreage in Bolivia, Peru, and Colombia, and the volume ratios involved in refining from leaf to paste, to base and the refined hydrochloride, respectively. These volumes of consumption are priced on the basis of the wholesale price for coca, assuming that Colombian traffickers have taken over control of most of this part of the operation.[13] The results demonstrate the minimum net income in dollars earned by the Colombian traffickers at each phase: it has been thought that a considerable part of the cocaine produced is lost; that the Colombians apparently only keep 65 percent of the wholesale value; that the Colombian traffickers do not act as retailers or run the crack houses in certain cities (which would double and even triple returns); and that the returns from marijuana are based on Colombian prices without taking into account the transporters and wholesalers inside the United States. It is thought that the Colombian traffickers take between 65 percent and 70 percent of wholesale income. Contained within those figures are the costs of transport and production, so this is in effect a net income figure.[15] In the case of marijuana, the amounts paid to farmers and local intermediaries stay within the country, with transport costs being assumed by the Americans. According to Bruce Bagley,[16] the recovery of Colombian marijuana sales is recorded by the DEA.

One can see how dealers have been able to flood the U.S. market in a very few years, bringing prices down considerably. Sheer volume of export has compensated for this price reduction, but it was more than offset by the establishing of the European market from 1987 onward. The sums that dealers have been accumulating are too high to be absorbed into the national economy. For this reason, as well as for ones of profit, they invest their surplus in the international markets. To give an idea of scale, estimated profits in 1989 were three times that obtained by the entire national manufacturing industry, including Ecopetrol.

Table 1
The Drug Trade and Colombia's Participation

Year	Weight	Average price kilo	US$	Colombian seizures	Marijuana	Totals in $US million
	(tons)	*(US$ million)*	*(million)*		*(US$ million)*	
1976	20	70	1,400	910	400	1,310
1977	30	70	2,100	1,365	500	1,865
1978	35	70	2,450	1,590	600	2,190
1979	40	70	2,800	1,820	500	2,320
1980	50	60	3,000	1,950	400	2,350
1981	70	60	4,200	2,730	300	3,030
1982	90	60	5,400	3,510	200	3,710
1983	100	50	5,000	3,250	170	3,420
1984	120	45	5,400	3,510	170	3,680
1985	130	40	5,200	3,380	110	3,480
1986	160	30	4,800	3,120	35	3,920
1987	200+30*	25	6,500	4,250	70	4,320
1988	230+40*	18	6,140	3,990	165	4,155
1989	200+50*	22	6,900	4,485	180	4,665

*Sales to Europe at US$50,000 per kilo

Source: Average wholesale prices taken from the General Accounting Office, "Drug Control in Colombia," 1988, quoted by Mauricio Reina, "Economía política y estrategia antidrogas: ¿Un esfuerzo fallido?" *Colombia Internacional*, no. 8 (Bogotá: Universidad de los Andes, October-December 1989). The quantities are derived from the same source, adjusted by the coefficients developed by Ethan Nadelmann between coca leaf, paste and base, less amounts lost in processing, transport, and interdiction. The 1989 figure estimate is based on reported large amounts seized (100 tons) and rise in prices.[14]

The Stockpile of Mafia Capital

Mafia investment has been in the estates around cities particularly where there is peasant unrest and guerrilla activity. The guerrillas had formed a huge T from east to west in the north of the country with a line running south, along the Magdalena River to the land settled by peasants. The drug baron landowners have managed to split the imaginary T with the collaboration of local landowners, the military, and their own forces, and so have achieved a privileged position within Colombian politics, one in which the extreme right has a very strong influence. It is estimated that the drug barons own nearly a million hectares out of a total of over 13 million hectares of farm land (or 4.3 percent of this).[17] The estimated value of the land alone would be equal to US$300 million, but for the more fertile lands, those close to cities, as well as additional investment in improvements, the total value might be triple that.

Part of "narco" livestock investment has gone toward breeding "pacer" horses and fighting bulls, but imported genetic technology and the construction of installations seem to have considerably increased livestock productivity. Luis Lorente points out that, in the last fifteen years, the use of breeding animals both for meat and milk in the lowland cattle ranches has become more common, as has the use of cattle as pack animals.[18] It is not possible to establish the global effect of such extravagant investment by drug traffickers, but there must have been some. All the above investment has kept the prices of live animals and meat stable over the last ten years.[19] However, the phenomenon has also caused those rural areas "cleaned up" by paramilitary groups to become overpriced: between the period 1982–1984 and 1989, the price per hectare in Puerto Boyacá rocketed from US$100,000 to US$1,000,000.[20] The impact that "narco" investment has in urban real estate is also noteworthy (see Table 2).

The drug mafias have also participated in banks, investments linked with multinationals, communication networks—radio (although the Cali cartel sold its Grupo Radial Colombiano to an evangelist group) as well as TV—chains of pharmacies, and some industries. It is impossible even to make an approximate calculation of these investments, given the use of frontmen and the level of secrecy in such transactions in the country. It has been estimated that mafia businesses within the country make up only a fraction of their dollar income. Very roughly, the average annual earnings of the Colombian cartels over the last ten years are in the order of US$4,000 million, of which US$1,500 million ends up in the country, the equivalent of 3.8 percent of the Colombian GDP.

Regarding employment, these illicit businesses contribute less than their share of GDP due to the livestock element. The coca plantations in the country have been calculated at some 40,000 hectares, which provide

Table 2
Real Estate Sales Attributable
to the Underground Economy

Year	US$ million
1979	323
1980	388
1981	609
1982	1,013
1983	547
1984	1,037
1985	700
1986	307
1987	425
1988	106
Total	5,455

Source: Borrero, "La finca raíz y la economía subterránea," November 1989.

120,000 jobs. Processing and refining are capital-intensive. Carriers, servants, and hired assassins would account for another 10,000 jobs. The marijuana plantations could provide employment for a further 60,000 workers, giving a total of about 190,000 (between 2 and 3 percent of the total estimated work force of 7,000,000 people).

Apart from the capital needed for the business itself, the amount invested in land and productive assets could reach a third of the earnings accumulated over ten years, which, with an annual interest of 5 percent on the same, would come to US$7,250 million. The figure calculated for the value of rural and urban property is US$1,000 million less and lends some coherence to the calculation of the entire amount of wealth contained within national borders.

Assuming a capital output ratio of 3:1 in the country and a GDP of US$40 billion this would indicate that the mafias own 6 percent of the total wealth of Colombia. The total financial capacity of the cartels would appear to be much greater, since they are supposed to have deposits in international banks and bond portfolios in the U.S. FED as well as that of other governments and shares worth around $35 billion, the equivalent of a third of the country's stock of capital, infrastructure, housing, and land. The domestic and foreign investments by this new layer of the bourgeoisie could mean that they own close to 40 percent of the wealth of all Colombians in and outside the country.

The Macroeconomy and Drug Trafficking

The inflow of US$1,500 million a year over the last ten years, with marked periodic variations, has had a major impact on the country's macroeconomic variables, particularly the balance of payments, fiscal accounts, and savings/ investment ratios. The existence of the black-market dollar over this period of time had various well-known effects: (1) a rise in imported contraband and the proliferation of distribution centers, the value of which in the 1970s was $US150 million and the current value of which stands at US$600 million; (2) the underinvoicing of imports, which is attractive to buyers because they pay part of the invoice in dollars at less than the official price and pay no taxes that could add up to 50 percent to the black-market price (estimated at around US$900 million a year); (3) overinvoicing of exports, possibly benefiting from a 14 percent government export subsidy for certain export items; and (4) counterpart for capital expatriated or external financing for changes in ownership of assets like land, apartments, and businesses. In the already quoted source by Borrero, it is estimated that the underground economy provides US$2.5 billion a year, of which US$1.5 billion comes from narcotics; the rest comes from smuggling both to and from Colombia (border trade) and remittances by Colombians living abroad.

From the above figures, we can see that Colombia does not export $5.5 billion, as the statistics say, but US$8 billion and that the GDP is not worth US$40 billion but US$46 billion if underground activities are included. While the legal GDP grew during the 1980s at a rate of about 3 percent a year, the underground GDP was able to grow by 7 percent, and this dynamism must in some way have affected legitimate trade. In this way, when it is said that the Colombian economy is highly protected and that a lowering of barriers is recommended, one forgets that contraband consumer sales may account for 15 percent of the sale of manufactured goods and far more of the sales of electrodomestic appliances and computers; by the same token, one forgets that a fifth of imports go unaccounted through the use of various ingenious mechanisms. In this way, the lowering of external trade and above all of financial barriers has been going on for fifteen years and is becoming more firmly established regardless of the legal measures applied.

Between 1978 and 1982, when there was a fairly ill-advised revaluing of the *peso*, the external black-market surplus combined with the legal surplus

Table 3
The Black Market and Official Dollar and the
Balance of Payments

Year	Black Market Premium over the Official Rate	Current Account Balance in Percent of the GDP
1970	12.0	−3.9
1971	11.0	−6.2
1972	5.9	−2.0
1973	6.2	0
1974	5.4	1.5
1975	−1.4	0
1976	−1.3	1.5
1977	−5.6	2.8
1978	−6.8	2.1
1979	−8.3	1.6
1980	−6.2	0.5
1981	−4.7	−3.7
1982	−0.7	−5.3
1983	11.1	−5.2
1984	13.8	−1.0
1985	2.2	0.6
1986	−0.3	1.3
1987	0.4	−0.2
1988	1.1	−0.9
1989	0.6 (Sept.)	−0.2

Sources: Banco de la República, "Informe mensual sobre tasas de cambio," and Dane and DNP for the balance of payments.

and contributed to the Dutch disease that was afflicting the country—financing and lowering the value of imports and making exports less profitable.[21] In the period that followed, however, when financing from abroad dried up and a growing part of available foreign exchange went toward servicing the foreign debt, the cushion provided by illegal income helped stop the economy from going bankrupt and helped stem capital flight, as experienced by the rest of Latin America, where it resulted in devaluation and hyperinflation.

As can be seen in Table 3, there exists a clear correlation between the positive or negative financial premium provided by the black-market dollar and the current account balance of the legal economy: a surplus in the current account is followed by a negative differential, and a deficit by a positive one. The record deficit of 1982, however, was followed by a black-market exchange rate that was a long way below the official value, and only when adjustment measures were taken did expectations lead to an overdemand in the black market in the three years that followed.

The cushion provided by the black-market-dollar surplus is exactly what guarantees the convertibility of capital working in the country into foreign exchange. Colombian professionals and business owners, according to a study by Gama Quijano,[22] have a total of US$18 billion deposited in the United States. These deposits had far-reaching consequences at the end of 1989 when the government disrupted some of the cartels' operations, causing a wave of violence that threatened the lives of countless businessmen, judges, journalists, and public officials.

One last point worth mentioning is that the fiscal balance has benefited from local investment by "narcos" looking to legitimize themselves and who, in the three tax amnesties over the last decade, have made significant tax contributions, such as the 0.3 percent of the GDP in 1987.

The Impact of the Antidrug Effort

The author believes that the cartels were momentarily disrupted by the 1989 campaign against them but that, as soon as things settle down, commercial and financial flows are simply rechanneled. The overwhelming advantage that the Colombians have is in their control of the wholesale cocaine market, extensive retail networks, and the sale of crack. The flow of foreign exchange continues for two basic reasons: first, the wholesale price of cocaine has increased by around 20 percent in various cities in the United States; and second, the mafias need more pesos to deal with the repression directed against them.

The impact on local mafia investment has been negative, since these were the businesses and properties most harassed by the authorities. There was a sharp drop in the prices of luxury real estate, and expensive cars not only began to sell at a discount but also were stopped by police and the army's street or highway patrols. Commercial establishments, restaurants, discotheques, and hotels suffered considerably due to bombs being planted at various key points. The Minister of Economy estimated that damage to private and public property and loss of business, was as much as 175,000 million pesos, in other words, 1 percent of GDP.

Most important of all is the fact that businessmen are pessimistic about the future, which has further restrained investment and speeded up the transfer of financial assets abroad, all in the face of a recession that was coming anyway. Servicing the foreign debt (55 percent of exports), the promise of further credit yet to arrive, fiscal policies, and high rates of interest have brought economic decline for over a year, accelerated by the slide in the international price of coffee in June 1989. The ambivalent campaign against cocaine trafficking leaves the economic future of the country looking even bleaker, comparable to the rest of the continent.

POLITICAL AND SOCIAL DIMENSIONS

Modern Penal Law and Imperial Puritanism

This section will support the view that legislation on drugs should take into account those principles that shape the modern penal system. As I will illustrate, drug legislation goes against the very structure that is formed around such principles. The recovery of these principles in drug issues could have undoubted liberalizing effects. This recovery also has the advantage of reaching diverse agreements fast since it is rooted in a legal, political, and cultural tradition. Those who seek radical transformation should not give up querying bourgeois penal law. Rather, the hope for transformation invites one to make the most of the progressive and democratic uses of those principles. Penal law regulates repression and punishment, and one tends to overlook the deep liberalizing effect that the modern penal system has.

We know the modern penal system as a political, legal, and cultural mechanism that, in its time, was a conquest of the bourgeoisie versus absolutism. As such, it had three new contributions to make: (1) the principle that no one can be punished without having committed an act exactly described in a law enacted prior to the execution of the said act; (2) prohibitions in the penal code should protect legal rights for society as a whole—the right not to be murdered, kidnapped, robbed, or swindled; (3) no one can be sentenced when, despite having committed an act typified under a penal code and having abused a legal right, the act occurred in circumstances for which a person cannot be validly reproached—in a demented state, for example.

The penal code revolves around these three premises, which act as limits against the punitive powers of the state. This overview becomes more evident if we imagine a state that did not have to act under any of these three restrictions, a situation that was a straightforward reality before the advent of the modern penal code.

The penal code is simply one of the devices that human societies have employed to control the reality—or the specter—of chaos. The penal code may be the most tried and tested mechanism but it is far from being exclusive. There are other—and perhaps better "designed"—ways of defining "deviant" human behavior and for ensuring control and punishment; these methods are still influential enough to be the bases of some social codes such as heresy or political dissent under certain regimes. Combatting these regimes becomes a confirmation of social cohesion and a legitimization of public powers as that cohesion's source and guarantee. Within this type of order, the precise definition of taboo behavior is irrelevant since it is the expression of an evil that is capable of constantly manifesting itself in a variety of forms. The important thing is to leave the authorities enough room for maneuvering to be able to eradicate the evil.

Nowadays, this kind of punitive regime seems obliged to act as if it were ashamed of itself, paying lip service to the written word of modern penal law. The result is confusion of the ideologies emphasizing perhaps the worst of both systems: the cold formality of the modern penal code, combined with the ambiguity and unpredictability of schemes of prohibition and sanctions. Today's prevailing rules on drugs, in Colombia and most of the rest of the world, reflect the nature of those schemes that we have just mentioned. Let us look at how they affect penal law in the case of Colombia.

Practically all crimes laid down in the National Statute of Narcotic Substances (1986 Law 30) deal with behavior related to "drugs which produce dependence." The statute defines three forms of dependence: "psychological dependence," "addiction or drug addiction," and "drug abuse (toxicomania)." But no mention is made of the substances that bring about these states. The interpretation of these crimes is left to the discretion of bodies who are far from sufficiently competent to dictate the law, bodies such as the Committee of Experts of the World Health Organization "for remitting international treaties approved by Colombia on the subject" or the health and/or legal medicine services in the country.

Specialists in penal law insist that description of criminal behavior ("penal types") should be in the most precise terms in order to guarantee legal security, which is the end of all penal law. But the National Statute of Narcotic Substances makes almost no attempt to do this. The "types" it lays down contemplate too many alternative forms of behavior: some open and imprecise, and others showing a lack of clarity between the wording and the circumstances contemplated by the same rules that increase or decrease the penalty.

Article 33 of Law 30, 1986 is a prime example of the first and most important of the characteristics mentioned, chanting a whole litany of alternative forms of behavior:

Whomsoever, without the permission of a competent authority, except in the use of an amount prescribed as being for personal use, introduces into the country, even in transit, or takes out from the same, transports, carries on his or her person, stores, keeps, prepares, sells, offers, acquires, finances or supplies in any form, a drug that produces dependence, will incur a prison sentence of four to twelve years and a fine of between 10 and 100 minimum wages.

Almost all the other forms of crime under the statute are similarly ill-defined and open to individual interpretation; these other forms of crime include real estate in some way linked to the production, marketing, or use of drugs; the stimulation and spread "in any way" of the use of the same; and the possession of materials that in any way could be used for drug production.

All these penal types equate, and establish the same punishments for, forms of behavior whose gravity would appear to be disparate: the production and sale of drugs that produce dependence, for example, is equated with the purchase and possession of drugs for personal use (in amounts exceeding a "personal dose"). In a famous ruling on 14 April 1980 (when the previous Statute of Narcotic Substances was in force), the Superior Tribunal of Medellin complained that judges had been sentencing "consumers who were not dealers for possession with the intent to consume, as if they were dealers." But it was the law itself that, when dealing with quantities that exceeded the so-called "personal dose," led the judges to treat consumers and dealers in the same way.

The National Statute of Narcotic Substances contains no definition of the legal right that it proposes to protect, and there is considerable disagreement among those who have attempted to define it. They have pointed to public health, the life and integrity of the individual, people's freedom to lead a normal life, peoples' economic rights, public safety, the survival of the state, public order, public economic order, the national economy, and the state's monopoly on drugs.

Public health is the most widely used argument, but it raises many questions, because it is not clear that someone who uses marijuana or cocaine, for example, is damaging anything more than his or her personal health. And if that is what the law seeks to protect, it does not seem feasible against the user's will. The contrary argument leads to the assumption that the health of individuals is in the hands of the state and not of the individual, which runs counter to modern penal law.

So these offenses are in the strange position of being in quest of a right which must be protected, because traditionally, in terms of the penal code, a clear collective agreement has been reached on certain social values (e.g., human life or property) which then defines the conduct of third parties who threaten those values (homicide or theft). Perhaps this is a form of reinforcement of prohibition. Prohibition attributes all drug-related activity to organized crime, which, in turn, performs all these activities with the same ruthlessness. This leads to the mistaken belief that the practices of growing, producing, selling, and using drugs offend against the same legal rights safeguarded by the classic legal norms of penal law that proscribe the crimes generally committed by drug smuggling gangs: homicide, personal injury, blackmail, bribery. The fact that these crimes are firmly rejected by society and call for repression by the state, however, does not justify perpetuating the confusion.

Article 87 of the National Statute of Narcotics establishes the following: "persons who, without having committed any of the described infractions in this Statute, are affected by the consumption of dependence producing drugs, shall be sent to the establishments referred to in articles 4 and 5 of decree 1136, 1970." In other words, such persons will be locked up and submitted to enforced treatment. Penal legislation has also stipulated "security measures," principally internment in psychological institutions, that require a number of conditions to be fulfilled for their application.

Here, however, we are dealing with an aberration—drug addiction—which alone would bring about the application of security measures: confinement and enforced treatment. The questions raised are not simply the result of "errors" in legislation when it comes to drugs, as one might assume. On the contrary, the questions reveal something structural. The laws on drugs are part of modern penal law, but they are deeply influenced by punishment schemes whose political, juridical, and cultural horizons are the antithesis of such law.

The original framework that shaped Colombian legislation on drugs, as well as that of many other countries, should be sought in the social, cultural, and political history of United States society at the turn of the century. It would be worthwhile to examine the role of puritanism in the formation of the American ethical/penal conscience. One should study other factors, such as the discrimination against racial and cultural minorities in the self-assertion of the identity of the people of the United States. The use of drugs has been associated, by average U.S. citizens, with certain ethnic minorities: opium with Chinese immigrants; cocaine with blacks; and marijuana with blacks and Hispanics. It would be wise to examine the role of these factors of national self-identification in legitimizing the role of the United States in the destruction/replacement of the colonial empires of a "decadent" Europe. Most important, however, is how the United States, with its growing power abroad, persuaded more countries to join its anti-drug crusade. From the International Opium Conference in Shanghai 1909, to the UN meeting that gave rise to the United Nations Convention against Illicit Traffic in Narcotic Drugs and Psychotropic Substances (Vienna in December 1988) and innumerable other international events, the leadership of the United States has been decisive, which has had two results: (1) the organization of nations has become a medium for the imperatives of the predominant ethical concepts in the United States on the issue of drugs; and (2) the legislation of a majority of countries has reproduced those imperatives.

The consequences only became important when a change of great historical significance took place—the change in outlook toward drugs by a large part of the U.S. population. What began as a somewhat rhetorical exaggeration of an essentially North American ethical approach for an international audience turned into a straightjacket for a large number of countries, because it provided international treaties and internal legal dispositions necessary to change the poor and weak countries, from which the drugs were exported, into launch pads in the war against drug trafficking.

Everything would seem to indicate that the social, political, and maybe even economic costs to these countries more than outstrip the benefits. For this to change, it would be essential for these countries to restate—with all due sovereignty—modern national penal codes. What are those values whose special meaning for the collective mentality calls for protection by penal law? How should the forms of behavior that infringe them be typified? How does one decontaminate national legislation from imperatives of ethics other than one's own and contrary to one's needs that exceed one's resources and distort the guarantees built, for good or for evil, into one's punishment systems?

Crime and Society in the Life of a Drug Trafficker

On 19 August 1983, the American Broadcasting Corporation (ABC) presented an hour-long documentary entitled "The Cocaine Cartel." In it, it was stated that "twelve families, mostly Colombian, direct the world trade in cocaine . . . cocaine and its profits have set in motion brutal killings committed by a new cast of organized criminals."[23]

The fact that the illegal cocaine trade was being run by Latin Americans was nothing new; nor was the celebrated barbarity of these criminals a revelation. In 1981, when the North American news agencies saw fit to dub them the "cocaine cowboys," the Dade County Public Security Department representative, Marshal Frank, claimed that "the mafia would do well to take a leaf out of the book of this more up-to-date breed of criminal. The Colombian underground are more prolific, better armed, and equally—if not better—organized and financed. Their objective is the same: the production, importation, and distribution of cocaine . . . and in the pursuit of these ends, human life has no value at all."[24]

This treatment is common to other publications. Writing to the *New York Times*, Richard Appleby, head of the New York narcotics section in 1981, claimed that it did not work "because Colombian drugs traffickers not only kill those people who testify against them, they would not hesitate to kill their own family. They are the most violent of drug smugglers."[25] Arthur Nehrbadss, ex-FBI crime specialist in New York and Chicago, in the same year added: "It is run like a family, like the Sicilian mafia, but when a member of the Cosa Nostra wants to kill someone he needs permission. Colombians point their machine guns and shoot."[26]

What is new in the ABC documentary is the idea of the unification of the clans and families involved in trafficking: from Bolivia through to the consumer, one single conspiracy. From then on, the following views were to be dominant in the United States: smuggling is controlled by Latin American foreign nationals who control 80 percent of the drugs consumed by the United States; most of these foreign nationals live abroad, and they have a system of blood ties similar to the Sicilian Mafia; they have formed themselves into regional cartels from which they agree on a policy to carry out their crimes in an organized fashion; their structure is hierarchical and controlled by codes of silence; and they are bloodthirsty and do not respect their own family.

Subsequent explanations followed later on to back up these views. For example, in 1987 the newspaper *Spectator* [El Espectador] announced that "The Medellin Cartel was formed on 18 April 1981, in Hacienda Veracruz belonging to the Ochoa Clan . . . the family met with Pablo and Carlos Correa, Carlos Lehder, and Rafael Cardona Salazar, among others, to devise strategies for the purpose of exporting cocaine to the United States."[27] Not infrequently, informers would link the cartels to governments hostile to the United States, like Panama or Cuba. This view was to dictate the policies for repressing the crime and separating allies from those hostile to the fight to eradicate or control it.

To present these criminals as members of cartels clearly serves the interests of U.S. strategy in dealing with the traffic, because this idea equates the different specialized stages of the growing and production of cocaine. The grower, the chemist, the hired assassin, or the pusher on the city streets are all tarred by the mafioso brush. They all participate in a crime (criminal conspiracy), from which a cause can be inferred.

The same approach places the heart of the problem abroad: since the main ringleaders and distribution networks are outside the United States, it is valid for the front of the offensive to be so also. This approach also suggests that the difficulties involved in capturing a member of the drug mafias are a result of the ties of complicity and corruption found outside North American society. U.S. police or functionaries are not to blame; the fault lies with corrupt communities in other small countries that are riddled with drugs and communism and that refuse to cooperate adequately with the strategy of repression. Once drug traffickers are captured abroad, the pressures for extradition produce certain benefits for the country in question.

This kind of reconstruction of the crimes involved hinders and obstructs the individual strategies of South American countries. The cartel theory is fundamentally a simplification of the phenomenon, it focuses on the transformation process leading up to consumption, and not on the later effects of the use of funds amassed by the business. The cartel theory is also what hinders the development of government policies that can effectively deal with the problem and, to the contrary, creates confusion over who should be pursued strategically.

The search for legitimate outlets and ways of laundering money by the cocaine barons "infects" the whole society presenting to the outsider the image of a drug-dominated country, while U.S. institutions that also reap the benefits and that have readily created channels for absorbing into society the heirs to these dubious fortunes are not analyzed.

The notion of the cartel so portrayed leads then to a minimization of the effects of the war on drugs. Since the ringleaders are hardly ever brought down or the nature of the business changed, it is felt that only the minor traffickers are caught and that there is a conspiracy to protect the bosses. When, as rarely happens, an important figure does fall, his humiliating removal to the United States and subsequent degrading treatment adversely affect the image of the government in the eyes of its citizens.

If the theory of the international drugs cartel does not help to realize policies and analysis, then it is necessary to look for models that do. With this criterion, and the inevitable arbitrariness of any classification and definition, I would like to propose a different notion of the kind of criminal associated with the cocaine trade.

Power Struggles Between Drug Cartels and Government

During the 1970s, Colombia became the world's largest producer of marijuana. The center of harvest and business transactions was in the region of La Guajira in the far north of the country. The total area under cultivation in this and other regions in 1979 was calculated at being between 100,000 and 300,000 hectares. Unlike today's cocaine trafficking, however, "the organization of transportation and financing between Colombia and the U.S.A. was definitely run by the North American mafia."[28]

It was the North American smugglers who came and proposed the business. They chose La Guajira as the final point of the Colombian side of the operation due to its position. It is the point nearest to the United States from Latin America, and its socioeconomic situation and the low level of government control made it the ideal jumping-off point. As the peninsula was not unpopulated, the business was built up on the existing social structure of the region: brotherhood (*compadrazgo*), family loyalty, blood codes, and a strange conception of death. Availing itself of this cultural tradition, the organization behind the cultivation did indeed style itself on the Mafia: five families controlled most of the shipments. To join these, what was needed were contacts (*compadres*) and a willingness to start at the bottom. The problem has therefore to do with this distortion of the traditional solidarity found in La Guajira: a good example is the blood feud between the Cardenas and Valdeblánquez families, which led to 150 deaths and provoked the intervention of important people in the process of conciliation.[29]

When the Americans found a source of marijuana of similar quality within their own territories, they closed down the Colombian connection for obvious cost reasons. Left to their own devices and with a step-up in crop extermination programs, most of the families opted to get out of the business and live off their memories. Only those organized in a more rational and up-to-date manner moved into the internal market, which was smaller and far less profitable.

Since the beginning of the seventies, there has been evidence of Colombian control over the processing and supply of cocaine. But this control had a different dynamic from the beginning: Colombian contacts this time are from inside the market and not from the growing end. Thus the main scenes of violence are on the streets of the United States; that is where the business is fought over. The years between 1970 and 1981 were characterized by a fierce campaign to dominate the market, which raised several questions. Was the need to use violence originally incited by the characteristics of the market itself? If the businesses had been run by individuals from a different country and cultural background, would the story be any different?

The hypothesis of the U.S. media is that the Colombians are inherently inhumane. Nevertheless, researchers tend to think that it is the special characteristics of illicit business that cause this violence, and not the nature of its protagonists; otherwise, other businesses run by Colombians, like coffee or the flower trade, would be run with a gun and the physical annihilation of competitors. However that may be, there are some businessmen who have gradually managed to consolidate their position and can dictate the rules of the game.

Why did these turn out to be Colombians and not Americans? The most common theory is that the Mafia in the United States were reluctant to get involved in drugs, whereas the inhuman cold-bloodedness of our fellow countrymen let them get right on with it. Thus the decision is attributed to individual and not objective factors, but that theory does not gel with the real attempts of organizations of Sicilian and Chinese extraction to get in on an operation worth millions or why other foreign businessmen have failed to remove the Colombians, despite violence or price wars.

What makes Colombian countrymen a special case and for the moment irreplaceable is Colombia's proximity to the grower countries on or near its borders, access to the Caribbean and the Pacific, and the numerous Colombian population in the United States.

Because of their cultural extraction, the series of phases within the production process, and the marketing conditions, the *coqueros*, or cocaine traffickers, took on a style of their own known as the *apuntada*. The *apuntada* permits that persons other than the original organizers participate according to their financial capacity or family connections. One of those implicated commented on the limited success of campaigns against it: "It is very hard to finish off the organization, simply because it does not exist. If someone is arrested or for any other reason loses his markets, his position is immediately taken by others."[30]

Thus markets are controlled through different channels, but the main channel is contacts: with retailers, with those who ease the way for imports, and so on. A crafty businessman can take each of these steps with a different partner, in order to profit with every jump in the price of the merchandise. The ideal is to start with a partnership in the coca paste and to end up selling the cocaine wholesale.

This is part of the role confessed by one of the very few persons who have agreed to comment on their activities related to the drug trade, Carlos Lehder:

I was the middleman, I would say, through the vast territories which I have facing the United States, a frontier, say, of 200 miles, to collaborate and help the Colombian bonanza for them to enter. . . . They used those territories the way they saw fit, and I gave them . . . the necessary protection. Never in my life have I had partners, but I met hundreds of persons. . . . The word mafia is something taken from Hollywood and pushed by the large newspapers to punish Colombians here.[31]

Thus the business has a deeper social pervasiveness. Not only criminals or family members can join. Multiple choices are available: investing partner, transforming chemist, "cook," transporter, mule, or bodyguard.

The first public information about life at the top of the drug business appeared in the 1980s. Not only did the press give drug barons headlines, but it also gave them some odd princely nicknames: the "Black Pope" of Coca, Benjamin Herrera Zuloeta; the Godmother of Coca, Martha Libia Cardona de Gaviria Montoya; the Queen of Coca, Marlen Orejuela Sánchez; or the other Godmother of Coca, Griselda Blanco.

Shootouts in grills and discos became famous, as did the purchase of sumptuous mansions at exorbitant prices with little legal paperwork. All this excess came to a head when those drug traffickers tellingly called "emergent" expressed an overt desire to integrate. This was the sign that the investment of the drug trade's profits had overflowed the private sphere of luxury consumption. By 1983, these drug barons were pressing for social integration and an acknowledgment of their prestige, via the quest for political control through community works and the generation of employment, and for the creation of a public, entrepreneurial image as multifarious investors. That was the aim of Carlos Lehder's Movimiento Latino, of Pablo Escobar's slum eradication campaign, of the Ochoa family's ostentation with "pacer" horses, and of Rodriguez Orejuela's emergence as a businessman.

The Colombian Government Responds

Everything seemed to be leading to a relative whitewashing and acceptance of the new class. In fact, in 1983 Carlos Lehder made declarations that openly praised the drug trade as an anti-imperialist campaign and announced his decision to accept the tax and social amnesties offered by President Belisario Betancur. This, however, was the drop that burst the dam of hegemonic social tolerance. Lehder was immediately subject to investigation, headed by the chief public prosecutor. The Church and politicians warned people against bowing to the new moguls.[32] This is how Daniel Samper Pizano, probably the most widely read columnist in the country, synthesized public judgment:

Several Colombians have been publicly accused of having amassed huge fortunes of dubious origin, and others, who like Mister Carlos Lehder, have confessed to their ties to the drug trade, have proved that they lack the virtue of patience. . . . They forgot to follow the golden rule, known to every good *mafioso*, that respectability is a fruit which takes at least a generation to ripen.[33]

The flashy newcomers quickly returned to clandestine activity and denounced several important persons for having profited from the money whose dubious origin they now so cruelly pointed out. President, ministers, politicians, bishops, and businessmen appeared on the list of narco-dollar takers. For one year, the hopes of legitimacy took the course of personal and clandestine bargaining. The central point in the dialogue was the drug traffickers' decision not to intervene in politics if the extradition treaty with the United States was not applied. The conversations continued even after Rodrigo Lara, Minister of Justice, was murdered, and President Betancur announced that he would extradite Colombian criminals wanted in other countries by producing a formal proposal to the government in June 1984.

According to reports made at the time, the only thing missing for the Colombian government to accept that proposal was agreement with the United States government. The highly suspect leak of the news by the American Embassy in Bogotá definitely jettisoned the agreement with the drug traffickers and revealed that the American government was not ready to accept non-extradition for cocaine traffickers. The failure of the negotiations and the continuation of the repressive measures in the country changed the outlook of the traffickers, who then had to opt between two strategies: increase their power locally or disappear.

Some of the traffickers, like Jorge Luis Ochoa and Rodríguez Orejuela, chose to disappear; they left their businesses secured and left the country. Others, like Pablo Escobar and Rodríguez Gacha, opted for the consolidation of a local power that would make them unshakeable, by upgrading gangs of bodyguards to real armies. They invested in land in areas of low state control, which provided ample possibilities for personalized solidarity systems. This second strategy met the local anti-subversive strategies devised by extreme-right landowners, politicians, and military officers that were intended to form strong blocks capable of forcing a guerrilla retreat and the dismantling of all forms of popular support for the left.

The mutual benefits in store made an alliance between the two sectors only a matter of time. One side put up the brains and guaranteed impunity, and the other contributed the money and the infrastructure. This context brought to the fore the right-wing paramilitary groups and the paid assassins (*sicarios*). From a group of bodyguards, the paramilitary groups became a permanent armed group for control over society and the elimination of potentially antagonistic groups. The *sicarios* became the hit men for the antisubversive alliance. Both phenomena have been attributed to the drug traffickers, because of the relation to money, but also because the traffickers changed the rules of the game when they added disproportionate defense costs to the business. In this way, control of the drug business became even more concentrated, and the use of the term *cartel* as an association started making sense. To belong to the Medellin cartel somehow meant counting on Pablo Escobar's military force, even if one did not receive orders from him.

A few years later, the drug traffickers declared that they had bought one million hectares, an act denounced as an agrarian counterreform that would seriously affect the structure of the Colombian countryside. The fact is that the basic illegal activity of the paramilitary and the *sicarios* had more to do with anti-subversion. It was anti-subversion and not cocaine traffic that produced the spiral of deaths and threats that have engulfed the country since 1984. The political winner was not the drug traffic, but the violent impulse of a specific type of society that is patrimonial, authoritarian, and non-communist, with intense social control over the people and belong-or-die relations. This is why action was taken not only against exponents of a radical change of system but also those who through their actions embodied a different society. The reasons for murdering someone were ideological and not the product of aggression toward the murdered.

The state tolerated this because it helped to maintain social control over a malcontent population. But the volume of the onslaught in areas where institutional action started being rejected generated a serious fracture in the state. The new offensive devised at the time had a clear defensive sign.

The call to war infers that the main responsibility lies with the cartels or international cocaine-traffic organizations. This point of view provides the basis for the ideology: drug traffickers are individuals with no nationality, narco-terrorists, merciless. So once again the focus is on the irrational or inhuman elements of the subjects, not on the objective conditions of the crime. The result is persecution in the form of an epidemic; anyone who has something to do with the drug trade is tainted by the above-mentioned atrocities. The organic concept of the cartel helps in making this type of action workable; from the following assumptions: (1) every drug trafficker belongs to a cartel; (2) the cartels are criminal organizations that generate violence; and (3) to belong to a cartel makes a person an accomplice of its actions. So every trafficker becomes co-responsible for violence because of his work, regardless of his real participation in violent acts.

In this way, the U.S. Drug Enforcement Administration (DEA) becomes central to the fight, since it is responsible for identifying those involved and making the extradition demands. And the search for the solution to a national problem ends up strengthening the American strategy. What remains is the factor that fostered the anti-subversive alliance or the moral or socioeconomic conditions that permitted the propagation of paid assassins. This is why it is necessary to go beyond the oversimplified cartel idea. This is the proposal of a strategic change in the approach to the issue. From the starting point proposed, there will be a more careful review of the relations between institutional crisis, counterinsurgency, and cocaine traffic. We may then discover that the enemies were not exactly the Medellin, Cali, Bogota or Atlantic cartels, or the ones that will go on being invented.

The Hypothesis of Repression

Until now we have been following the effects of a determined plan of action. It would be reasonable to ask what the effects of this argument are for general repression:

The repression paradigm is the complete rejection of any behavior that involves drugs. Commonly used forms have been prohibition, repression, punishment, fear, the dark consequences of drug abuse (perversion, delinquency, illness), the use of labels which describe the drug addict in such a way as being unreformable and irretrievable, the tendency to isolate the phenomenon and the people involved therein, and the different treatment given to legal and illegal drugs.[34]

There are many authors who tend to consider that this approach has failed, given the growing increase in, and social acceptance of, consumption in spite of campaigns, the destabilizing effect of campaigns in the Third World, and the need to fight the use of drugs with methods different from the ones envisaged in penal law.[35]

Other more perceptive authors maintain that international repression will only stop once the United States has produced a synthetic drug with similar characteristics to cocaine.

A view that hopes to distance itself from sensationalism and manipulation, unfortunately also tends to reduce the importance of the problem. This is frequently the case with analyses which look at it from a largely economic point of view, for example. One illustration of this is the one that presumes that the cocaine issue is a Latin American business that is eroding the U.S. economy, arriving at the conclusion that once the North Americans control the trade then the whole thing can be sorted out without further ado. This type of reasoning becomes more acceptable when one takes into account the marijuana trade.[36]

Both points of view also have in common the fact that they focus on the relationship between cocaine production and its consumption. In Colombia, however, far more importance is attached to the interplay between repression and efforts to come to terms with the conduct and illegal activities of the traffickers after the sale of the product. It is from this point of view that we will try to measure the success or failure of repression.

Drug trafficking did not bring about the breakdown of justice. On the contrary, it is nothing new, and it has often been quoted as one example of the limitations of democracy. The question suggested as being at the heart of the matter is this: "Given the increasing socioeconomic complexity of recent times, are the courts and magistrates capable . . . of dealing with class conflict and mass transgressions of the law involving whole groups and communities?"[37] The question about the administration of justice is over-shadowed by other points: the slow pace at which it moves, its inefficiency, the lack of resources. Perhaps the very illegality of drug trafficking is what reveals the crisis in all its intensity. Let us look at what is called the law of the two metals for officials: silver or lead.

For a few years, people complained of the corrupt judges who were bought by the dealers, but, in fact, this is only one aspect of the power over institutions achieved by local strongmen. This corruption is nothing new in Colombia: a large part of the political structure works in a similar fashion. What was different in this case was that the evidence was more obvious and was in opposition to views of other powers that be. But, the central issue, the administration of justice, did not lose its own particular bias.

Later on, with the assassination of magistrates and judges a daily reality, people began to speak of the fragility of the whole structure. Under normal circumstances it is assumed that one can rely on a judge because he or she maintains the monopoly of power and because he or she is backed by a consensus that vindicates his or her decisions. If this assumption is questioned, the judge's decisions need to be reinforced by the other branches of the establishment. This added support lessens the likelihood of an independent decision.

Thus the judiciary was caught in a paradox: much of the solution to its institutional crisis lay in its independence as an effective power, that is to say, in its autonomy to judge crimes and noninterference by other bodies (military, executive, congressional) in passing judgment. But this independence is questioned by real bullets, and the judges feel obliged to request the collaboration of the institutional structure, which implies conditions, given the warlike nature of the offensive.

The campaign of repression does nothing for this judicial branch of the establishment but weakens it by exposing its gaps. The judiciary is unable to satisfy military and executive expectations of quick, summary guilty verdicts. But if it does not, it is the judicial branch at the forefront of the crisis or suspected of partiality. The judiciary does not want to lose the role assigned to it by the constitution, but it is forced to admit that other bodies have to take over its functions because of the unsustainable cost of repression.

What is more, the idea of total war against the drug trade would really relegate the judiciary to the sidelines. If there is war, the other side becomes the enemy and must be defeated. This idea is incompatible with modern penal theory, which does not see the criminal as an enemy nor punishment as the vengeance of society. For all these reasons,

the crisis of the judiciary should be put in a different context. . . . For structural reasons an efficient judiciary is not yet possible. Efficiency implies a certain rigidity in terms of social control. Inefficiency is the way it operates, one way of making the judiciary's functions more flexible. In the long run, its inefficiency will be a prerequisite for the emergence, justification and development of new forms of social control.[38]

Everything would seem to point to the fact that the regime strengthens its position with the repression hypothesis, even when some of its institutions lose credence.

We have looked at the effects on the structure of the ordinary system of justice. The political class is also offended, since a large chunk of its power is tied up with the backing of business capital and the old-boy network. On the other hand, the executive and the military do rather well out of the measures; the former because it has managed to legitimize itself, the second because it has partly restored its monopoly on the use of force. The so-called war on drugs, in spite of the blessing it has received from the Supreme Court, has based itself on two realities clearly alien to ordinary situations—seizure and extradition. The first reality concerns the confiscation of goods presumed to have been procured with money from drug dealings, which meant stretching the law governing the confiscation of property used in the perpetration of a crime (Law 30 of 1986, article 47). In other words, suspected illicit gain or an accusation by the DEA gives rise to the assumption that property was obtained through drug trafficking and, as such, is liable to temporary seizure—an idea in contradiction to the principles of penal law.

Administrative extradition is also an exception. The original source was the Reciprocal Convention on Extradition of Accused Persons signed in 1888 with the United States, approved by Law 66 of the same year, and broadened in the Additional Convention adopted in 1943 by Law 8.

In accordance with the rules herein, the procedure agreed by the two states for handling extradition requests in the aforementioned treaties, is exclusively administrative, without the need for any participation on the part of the countries' judicial authorities . . . it is for the government to decide, exclusively and absolutely its own discretion, whether it agrees to the petition or rejects it.[39]

It would seem impossible to launch a campaign as the government did with the announcement of 18 August 1989, without invoking special powers, but it seems relevant that the government should invoke these special powers, thus distancing itself from the channels of the institutions already in place. The crux of the matter, however, is the institutionalization-flexibility dichotomy of social control. As we have shown, the so-called dirty war served the state's interests in terms of social control; however, it is no longer completely functional and must find other forms of expression.

The transition cannot be made via ordinary institutions because they have had to suffer, serve, and put up with the way things were before. For the same reason, however, relations worsened with the legislature and the judiciary, where it is not possible to bring about automatic change. In this context, the location of the battle becomes a key issue. If the struggle is against organized criminals who generate violence, any action is justifiable because it supports institutions.

From this perspective, the repression hypothesis has worked. It remains to be seen whether it can be maintained continuously. The government and the military have announced that no quarter will be given, but with the death of the ring-leader Rodriguez Gacha and the intervention of public figures, the direction of the offensive may be changed and its effects become less severe.

From another point of view, since the conditions that generate the dirty war or armed counterinsurgency against potentially hostile groups are not affected, the struggle will be carried on through other allied groups in accordance with local circumstances. There is also the risk that the establishment, faced by the need for irrational social control, may again try and distract attention toward other actors in society. For some, the more obvious signs are already present in the form of a new offensive against the armed insurgency of the left, which is front-page news.

The Search for Alternatives

As has been said, the subject of alternatives involves the various phenomena that go beyond drug trafficking, especially (1) social control; (2) the issue of drug trafficking as a business; and (3) Latin American leadership. First, we refer to social control, central to the whole situation. It is important to stress the factors that make the creation of an antisubversive or counterinsurgent alliance possible.

A social scheme should be designed to eliminate the factors that have led to the current state of affairs. As can be inferred, it would suggest a strategy that would create a new institutionality as well as local ethics. Urgently needed is a reordering of both the local powerbase and the way in which drug money has been invested in it. Possible steps toward this restructuring might be the dismantling of armed groups and the opening of regional discussions, socialization that influences the culture of death and reputation that has provoked the outbreak of hired killers in the inner cities and the creation of effective controls on the investment of money destined to corrupt institutions or turn them into private instruments.

Second is the issue of drug trafficking as a business, with both a long-term strategy and temporary measures. The long-term strategy includes elements like the need for the international legalization of the consumption of cocaine or, at least, its gradual decriminalization. Associated factors would be economic measures to ensure that legalization did not damage the fragile links in the chain (growers, those employed in the refining and those who make their living from other legal *coquero* enterprises). Factors like the monopoly of the market, subsidized agriculture or profitable crop substitution acquire new significance.

There should be several temporary measures. First, the phenomenon should be better defined. Criminal involvement should be differentiated and a system for judging cases in Colombia established. Profits made from drug trafficking should also be differentiated, and criminal involvement in drug money laundering practices. This would be an integrated approach, recognizing all the stages in cocaine production, and would lead to differentiated treatment of the sale and processing of the drug in its earlier stages. It is equally necessary, given the level of current conflict with some of the implicated drug dealers, for civil society to be directly involved in proposing concrete measures and adequate conditions for judging crimes committed in the past and in searching for commitments that will counter the participation of the *coqueros* in the dirty war.

Third, in searching for alternate solutions to deal with the problem, pressure must come from a block of Latin American countries. What is important is that the policies applied be advantageous to the producer countries. The group should focus on policies for dealing with the most pressing problem: the existence of owners of vast fortunes in impoverished countries.

Drug Trafficking and Human Rights Abuses

Abuses of human rights have resulted from several major causes in Colombia. In addition to assassinations and attacks on property in Colombia, large numbers of Colombians have had to resign from their jobs and leave the country when faced with the imminent threats of kidnapping, torture, or death to their families and themselves. The resulting insecurity and lack of tranquility is not limited to Colombia, since countrymen could be attacked by hired assassins or drug dealers abroad. Moreover, to violence and death threats, add blackmail, infiltration, and bribery of administrative and judicial authorities as well as of the armed forces, criminal acts that have corrupted a large portion of public and private powerbases. A growing number of military and police officials have been investigated and disgraced because of links with drug trafficking; numerous politicians, public employees, and directors of private companies have been investigated or suspected of links with drug trafficking. In addition, many officials have been connected to criminal paramilitary and political actions of the far right. Finally, the

Colombian authorities themselves have expedited and reformulated certain penal norms and procedures that restrict Colombian human and civil rights; the authorities have proposed many operations in which human rights have been abused.

The Crimes of the Mafias. The most common and serious form of human rights abuses are the daily killings and the terrorist attacks that occurred with terrifying frequency in the last quarter of 1989. These events have seriously disrupted Colombian society and the state and could provoke the emergence of a totalitarian regime. The assassination of a minister of justice, Rodrigo Lara Bonilla, on 30 April 1984, can be added to that of the owner of the newspaper *El Espectador*, Guillermo Cano, and more than forty journalists in five years; that of the director of the antinarcotics police, Col. Jaime Ramirez, and more than 1,300 operatives; that of a court magistrate, Hernando Baquero Borda; that of Jaime Pardo Leal, national president of the Union Patriotica; that of a prosecutor general of the nation, Carlos Mauro Hoyos; that of the governor of Antioquia, Antonio Roldan; and that of a candidate for the presidency of the Liberal Party, Luis Carlos Galan.

To these assassinations of well-known figures can be added the deaths of thousands of defenseless citizens who have lost their lives in this war against drug trafficking. Economic losses have skyrocketed. Industry, commerce, and the informal economy calculate the physical damage by the attacks that followed the death of Galan, a presidential candidate, at around 1,742 million pesos, and a further loss of 60 billion pesos in sales. In all, the official calculation is that drug-related violence (at its worst in 1989), together with guerrilla activity and crime, prevented a generation of wealth estimated at around 170,000 million pesos, the equivalent to the one point of growth that the 1989 GDP should have experienced (4.5 percent).

According to the Asonal Judicial Union, between 1980 and 1989, 261 judges and magistrates had been murdered (71 of whom fell in the Barco administration), and 80 percent of these murders resulted from investigating events involving the *capos* (bosses) of the mafias in cases of violence against journalists, politicians, peasants, and judges. After the assassination of the minister Lara Bonilla, for which—on the orders of Judge Tulio Manuel Castro Gil, who was himself murdered in Bogotá 23 July 1985—Pablo Escobar Gaviria was among those investigated, the death threats have been unending, causing the exile of two public attorneys. An old indictment of Escobar for the murder of three members of the judicial police in 1975 cost the life of the magistrate Gustavo Zuluaga Serna.

The top bosses of the Medellin cartel were linked as instigators of the massacres at Urabá, Mejor-Esquina, Piñalito, Segovia, El tomate, and so on, working in close collaboration with the armed forces, after which warrants for the arrest of the officers and subofficers were issued and many investigations opened. The second judge of Public Security, Martha Lucia Gonzalez, who issued the warrants, had to leave the country after repeated death threats. Her father was then murdered, as was the third judge of Public Security, Maria Elena Diaz Perez, to whom it was left to continue the investigation and who refused to revoke the warrants for arrest. Of the 4,600 judges in the country, 1,600 (34 percent) have received death threats from mercenaries or paramilitary units in the pay of the drug traffickers. To be a penal judge in Colombia is considered a high-risk profession.

Thanks to the economic resources that they can count on, the drug cartels are equipped with the latest portable weapons. They have hundreds of AR-15 rifles, a weapon manufactured by the United States for the best shots in the navy; A-47 machine guns—similar to the AR-15s and the most sophisticated available assault weapons of European manufacture; mini-Uzi-submachine guns and Galil rifles, both of Israeli manufacture; pistols and revolvers of various calibers; fragmentation and rifle grenades; dynamite; rockets; and bulletproof jackets. The drug runners also have at their disposal hundreds of aircraft and light planes as well as dozens of helicopters, hundreds of hidden airstrips and helipads, and even a port situated in "El Meson de las Margaritas," located between Cartagena and Tolu on the Atlantic coast through which arms, ether, and other chemicals have been introduced into the country from abroad.

It is common for there to be tunnels linking the drug dealers' estates to roads or other estates as well as complex sentry systems using sophisticated communication technology that permit prompt detection of the arrival of a plane or car. There are usually secret storage areas where there are hidden on occasion large amounts of arms and explosives for supplying their armies or for attacks, and cellars with chains and shackles in the wall to hold kidnap victims.

The Involvement of the Military in Drug Trafficking. The involvement of the military in the drug mafias represents one of the most serious threats to a constitutional state and, of course, to the rights and liberty of the citizens. Via the military and police personnel of all ranks involved in the business, the mafias are able to use and maintain laboratories and transport drugs throughout the country and abroad, but they also enjoy immunity for their crimes, by receiving advance warning of police operations. These security forces also act as an armed wing for the mafia cartels, which is how Pablo Escobar and other *capos* have avoided capture on a number of occasions.

The State of Cordoba military and police chiefs, along with their counterparts from Puerto Escondido, received monthly payments upwards of 20 million pesos to guarantee the use of a hidden airstrip, from which tons of drugs are exported to the United States. "It is not a result of lack of military capability that the big drug traffickers have avoided capture," stated the prosecutor general of the nation on 18 December 1989, referring to the infiltration by the "narcos" of the security forces, "but because they have informants in the police and the army who warn them in advance when operations supposed to lead to their arrest are undertaken."

Under pressure from the DEA, the cleaning up of the security forces to eliminate those elements linked to drug trafficking began during 1989. In the first nine months of 1989, 877 agents had been dismissed for misconduct (3.2 per day), including 45 officers and 60 junior officers of the police; and 14 officers, 169 junior officers, and an undetermined number of ordinary soldiers of the armed forces; in all a significant number for links with drug trafficking. The dismissals ranged from the director general of the police, General Jose Guillermo Medina Sanchez, to hundreds of ordinary police.

Bribery and Other Methods. In addition to murder, other practices common to drug traffickers to evade justice are threats, blackmail, and bribery of the administrative, police, judicial and prison authorities, who on numerous occasions have helped offenders to escape trial, to avoid going to prison, or to break out of jail. Through questionable judicial practices or bribery, well-known drug trafficking *capos* have managed to remain at large, for example, Jorge Luis Ochoa, due to a writ of habeas corpus obtained by his lawyer, a one-time court magistrate, or the Honduran Matta Ballesteros, due to having spent millions bribing his guards in "La Picota" prison.

Faced with the failure of murder and terrorist attacks aimed at thwarting the operations of the authorities, the former creators of the paramilitary group "Death to Kidnappers" (*Muerte a Secuestradores*, or MAS) have themselves resorted either to abduction as a weapon to safeguard the life or freedom of their members, or even to entering into discussions with the authorities. The kidnappings of commercial and industrial figures—even of relatives of President Barco—served to open negotiations that have led to the freeing of the detainees with an apparent admission of defeat by the "extraditables," that was accompanied by the surrendering of a busload of a metric ton of dynamite. In spite of the merriment this incident caused and its initial rejection by the government, President Barco stated that the government is not "inflexible." Dialogue through intermediaries, as had happened before the death of Galan, might turn out to be promising.

The "narcos" have at their disposal, what is more, an extensive intelligence network with informants in all branches of public administration and the armed forces, as was revealed by the documents leaked about the one-time captain Jose Wanumen. This network included informants with access to highly classified information from the Ministry of Justice, the government, and the Ministry for Foreign Affairs relating to action taken against drug trafficking and negotiations on extradition to the U.S.A., from documents of the National Council of Narcotic Drugs, from the judicial police and the State Prosecutors Office records departments.

Paramilitary Groups. General Maza Marquez stated that the paramilitary groups, as they are known today in Colombia, are the result of what the drug traffickers have interpreted as self-defense. The paramilitary groups, which originated in the policy of self-defense created by the army as a result of the martial law decree No. 3398 in 1965 (later Law 48 of 1968) as a strategy to involve citizens in the fight against guerrillas, became the private armies of the mafias during the 1980s without ever abandoning either the purpose for which they were originally created—that is, counterinsurgency—or contact with the army.

The paramilitary groups were joined by bands of hired assassins. Some were hired by the drug traffickers for "jobs" (especially in Medellin), and others like MAS [the "Death to Kidnappers" group], were set up at the start of 1981 by the main drug traffickers meeting in Cali that put up an initial sum of 28 million pesos for the formation of a commando unit to free Marta Nieves Ochoa (sister to the drug trafficker Jorge Luis Ochoa, kidnapped by members of M-19 who were brutally murdered in order to obtain her freedom). An investigation carried out by the State Prosecutor's Office in 1983 revealed that 59 active military personnel were involved in the activities of MAS.

Those hired for "jobs" are responsible for most of the 142 massacres that have caused 1,193 deaths from 1988–89. Groups like MAS are the authors of most of the political crimes which have taken place in the cities. Altogether there are 150 groups who have operated and still do so all over the country. In a confidential report by the Security Administration Department (DAS) dated 20 July 1988, it was stated that

the hired assassins and the drug traffickers who operate in the vicinity of Puerto Boyaca (Boyaca) use the Association of Peasants and Farmers of Magdalena Medio (ACDEGAM) as a front. This organization has more than 300 armed men at its disposal spread throughout the municipalities of Puerto Boyaca and Otanche (Boyaca), Cimitarra and Puerto Olaya (Santander), La Dorada (Caldas) and Puerto Berrio (Antioquia), with an established infrastructure that includes more than 100 vehicles, including jeeps, pickups, cars, trucks, and light airplanes.

The group is maintained by drug traffickers, farmers, and peasants who to varying extents use part of their land for the cultivation of coca; activities disguised by other legitimate agricultural practices. Each one of those people periodically donates a quota of anywhere between 50 thousand and a million [pesos] to finance the band of hired killers.

Some authorities with jurisdiction in Magdalena Medio collaborate with ACDEGAM in particular the following: the regional prosecutor of Honda (Tolima), the commander and assistant commander of the Puerto Calderon military base, the police commander of La Dorada (Caldas region), the police commander of Puerto Boyaca, and Luis Rubio, Mayor of Boyaca (today a fugitive from justice), who is purported to "receive the sum of 2 million pesos a month from the drug traffickers."

According to the same report, the band of criminals known as MAS is subsidized by the Medellin cartel, who own some rural properties in the Magdalena Medio area. There are a number of assassination schools in these same areas, and large coca plantations and sophisticated laboratories for the treatment of the alkaloid. MAS is the oldest and most extensive of the paramilitary organizations, with branches throughout the country, responsible for hundreds of murders. In the Magdalena Medio assassination schools, the presence of Israeli, German, English, and North American instructors was revealed. Assassins wages varied from 30 to 40 thousand pesos when they graduated; this monthly amount was slowly increased according to the scale of the missions assigned by the *capos*.

Since February 1988, the instructors in the service of the drug traffickers and farmers trained more than 200 assassins and paramilitary operatives out of an army of more than a thousand men. That is how the men of Fidel Castaño were trained; Castaño was head of the Ochoa clan's strike force, a branch of the Medellin cartel, who was linked to the massacres at Amalfi (18 people), Currulao, Turbo, Uraba (20 banana plantation workers), and Mejoresquina (38 peasants) and owned farms in Uraba, Magdalena Medio, and Cordoba. In Magdalena Medio, as was admitted by Col. (retired) Luis Bohorquez, ex-commander of the Barbula battalion based in Puerto Boyaca, the organization, promotion, and protection of the private armies in the service of the drug traffickers was achieved with the backing of the law and the direct orders of his superiors. The paramilitary recruited their personnel above all from the remote villages or from the lower end of the class structure.

In June 1989, a supposed peasant called Luis Antonio Ramirez declared himself overall commander of the Magdalena Medio private armies. He stated that under his command there were 100,000 men organized in peasant fighting groups and that he was able to call up some five thousand men at a moment's notice to fight the guerrillas. Subsequently, the army's press office revealed Ramirez's true identity: he was actually ex-army captain Leon Guillermo Tarazona, who had been dismissed in November of the previous year for misconduct and who had links to the Medellin cartel and the assassin schools of Magdalena Medio.

The paramilitary groups established a solid base in Magdalena Medio, which they hoped to impose as an example of social order in other parts of Colombia. However, their vehemence, which led them to attack not only left-wing and popular organizations but also judges and state security personnel brought about their persecution on the part of the government. Twenty-four assassin schools had been established in the country.

Responses by the Authorities. During 1989 the drug traffickers received a beating at the hands of the Elite Corps of the National Police created in April 1989 and made up of 800 specialized commando units. This Corps has a tally of 3,500 raids; 2,000 arrests; 40 criminals killed; and 50 laboratories destroyed; as well as the capture of Jesus Baquero Agudelo (alias "Vladimir"), the author of 74 assassinations and 4 massacres; and the death of Rodriguez Gacha. The Corps has seized 350 motorcycles and cars, 60 planes, 125,000 gallons of liquid inputs and 62,500 rounds of ammunition.

On 1 September 1989, the Security Administration Department (DAS) evaluated operations against drug trafficking during the first eight months of 1989:

suspects arrested—12,861;

kilos of cocaine seized—21,941;

kilos of coca base captured—11,524;

kilos of dried and pressed marijuana confiscated—425,524;

coca crops destroyed—378;

laboratories destroyed—288;

airstrips out of action—62;

vehicles requisitioned—1,543;

launches—42;

planes held—359; and

properties occupied—464.

In January 1990, the Fourth Brigade captured 103 members out of 58 bands of assassins, and DAS arrested 18 assassins responsible for 48 separate murders and 5 massacres. Despite these successes, these groups are still operational. On 14 January 1989 a paramilitary unit from Fidel Castaño's organization descended on Pueblo Bello (between Turbo and Pueblo Nuevo) and carried off 42 of its inhabitants, mostly peasants sympathetic to the Patriotic Union (UP) and the People's Front (FP). Although there is an army camp on the road by which the kidnappers came and went, to date nothing is known of their fate.

Drug Wars. Violent confrontations between the cartels of Cali and Medellin remain another serious threat to law and order. These clashes seemed to have originated when the Medellin cartel tried to take over the

New York cocaine market, which had traditionally been managed by the Cali cartel, and when the former tried to involve itself in the latter's affairs.

Terrorist attacks, assassinations, theft of property, and abduction of members of either cartel have also caused deaths and property damage outside the conflict. By August 1989, drug wars had resulted in the loss of over one thousand lives, 52 dynamite attacks, 200 buildings damaged, and material losses amounting to a billion pesos. In 1989, there were 42 dynamite attacks on stores belonging to the *Drogas La Rebaja* drugstore chain and the Grupo Radial Colombiano (reportedly owned by Rodriguez Orejuela), which caused damage worth more than three billion pesos.

Some of the drug traffickers, like Gonzalo Rodriguez Gacha, learned about crime in the "emerald" traffic mafia, the guild that started the private armies and *vendettas* between mafia groups that were later to surface within the drug cartels and between the drug and emerald cartels.

The war between the *esmeralderos* and the drug mafias for the control of the mines, often under a single *don*, has caused hundreds of murders and dozens of massacres. Both Victor Carranza, whose farms in Puerto Lopez in the state (departmento) of Meta, were used for clandestine cemeteries and training grounds for paid assassins, and the late Gilberto Molina have been repeatedly singled out by the authorities as *esmeralderos* and drug traffickers. Molina was murdered in Sasaima together with twenty of his bodyguards and friends apparently on the orders of his ex-partner Rodriguez Gacha. Rodriguez Gacha has also been held responsible for six attacks against Tecminas and other firms in the emerald business, causing millions in losses and the death of sixty-one emerald traders in 1989 alone.

Actions Against Social Reform. One way of laundering drug money has been investment in land and real estate, which the mafia is supposed to have acquired to the value of US$5.5 billion. Two weeks before the murder of Luis Carlos Galan, the Partido Liberal's candidate for the presidency of the republic, government security had identified seven hundred properties registered by the drug cartel. Carlos Arturo Marulanda, at that time minister of development, revealed that the drug trade contributed one point to the growth of the gross domestic product, then reckoned at 4 percent a year. The land acquired by the drug traders is calculated at one million hectares, which concentrates wealth even more. This is twice the land expropriated by the agrarian reform institute, INCORA, over twenty-five years, and amounts to a counterreform larger than the state's.

Through self-defense, paramilitary efforts, or assassins, the drug traffickers have been murdering peasants and trying to stop the reform efforts of INCORA. These actions were denounced by Carlos Ossa Escobar, head of INCORA, at the XII World Environment Conference held in Cartagena in May 1989. At the Amazon Summit held in Brazil, President Virgilio Barco denounced the efforts of the drug trade to promote uncontrolled colonization in the jungles of Colombia and neighboring countries, one of the main causes of deforestation and destruction of the ecosystem, notably in the Amazon basin. He also denounced the U.S. government's practice of spraying coca and marijuana crops with the herbicides paraquat and gliphosphate. The drug traffickers, through ACDEGAM, have come out in defense of the right-wing paramilitary project and created the Movimiento de Restauracion Nacional (MORENA); however, accusations by the Security Administration Department (DAS) have prevented the movement from attaining legal status.

The drug trade identifies with the capitalist system, to which it is tied by common interests. Drug traffickers have become landowners, cattle breeders, industrialists, retailers, and real estate owners, all of which pitches them against social reform. For years, drug traffickers have been allies of the most reactionary sectors in the army in the fight against subversion and the popular movement. Under the pretense of a dialogue with the government and social forces, they aim to stifle social dissent and the guerrilla movement and to promote respect for their private property, which makes them a potential danger for the popular movement.

Abuses by the State. Genocide, assassinations, and terrorist attacks have influenced public opinion (out of 619 persons interviewed by the Nacional Consulting Center in August 1989, 70 percent were in favor of the death sentence for paid assassins) and strengthened the tendency toward hard-line political and legal measures and toward the state's military buildup. The seriousness of the public order problem has been used as justification for norms that curtail citizens' rights and freedoms. Proof rests in the antiterrorist statute, decreed immediately after the murder of the Attorney General, Carlos Mauro Hoyos, and the dozens of state-of-emergency decrees that typify new crimes and restrict procedural and constitutional guarantees, like *habeas corpus*, reverse the burden of the proof in the cases of expropriation of drug traffickers, lengthen the remand period in preliminary criminal investigations, extend the powers of the judiciary police to the military, and extend the extradition of Colombians to other countries by executive procedure.

Thousands of persons have been victims of brutal military raids, have been held in prison for weeks, or have had their property taken away. In the days following the murder of the Liberal Party presidential candidate, Galan, 10,450 persons were arrested.

In 1989 the national director of criminal investigations denounced repeated military and police interference in judiciary inquiries into drug trafficking or other crimes committed by their men, actions recently denounced by judges in Cali. Twenty-two political representatives and mayors of the Magdalena Medio, who are supposed to monitor human rights, support and defend (as was made evident in a forum held in Puerto Boyaca in June 1989) the forming of the "self-defense" or paramilitary bands responsible for hundreds of violations of human rights (tortures, mass murders, disappearances, etc.).

Members of the armed forces have occasionally acted as muscle for the drug trade, as happened last July 5 when the Altos del Portal building was raided and four people inside murdered. The army was trying to kill *esmeraldero* and Drug Enforcement Administration (DEA) informant Angel Gaitan in an operation that had been organized by Rodríguez Gacha. Three officers (one major and two captains) and three non-commissioned officers (sergeants) were found responsible and then dismissed by the state prosecutor.

The Ministry of Justice has become a ministry for the repression of drug traffic, which is where most of its budget goes. And close to half of the Security Administration Department (DAS) expenses, which should go toward fighting the various types of criminal offenses that afflict Colombians, go to pay the bodyguards of over 3,000 public officials and members of political parties.

The military budget has been severely readjusted over the past two years: it went from 177,070 million pesos in 1988 to 344,220 million pesos in 1989. Today it represents one-quarter of the national budget, which has meant slashes in the social budget.

Violations of Sovereignty. The fight against drug trafficking has been used to intervene in the country's internal affairs, violate national sovereignty, interfere with Colombian foreign trade, and harass Colombians abroad. American military aid has increased, with US$65 million delivered in military equipment that has been used more against the guerrillas than against the drug trade. Eighty-five percent of this "aid" was for the army and the air force. Miguel Gomez Padilla, director of the national police, declared that "aid" was inadequate to fight the drug trade.

According to the Pentagon, fifty to one hundred military advisers will be sent into Colombia and will not get involved in combat but will shoot back if shot at; however, the military advisers have already been spotted in combat areas against the guerrillas (as in the recent bombings in Yondo, department of Antioquia). In April 1988, the U.S. Drug Enforcement Administration also had 135 officers in Colombia.

Extradition of Colombian nationals is done through the executive branch (and the power of martial law) and not the judiciary, although the supreme court of justice declared inapplicable the law that enacted the extradition treaty. Colombians sent to the United States are judged in trials that violate judicial equality before the law (in a climate of xenophobia); they are judged for actions that are not crimes in Colombia and given sentences that do not exist there, like life imprisonment. Extradition is an indispensable tool to fight impunity, but it is essential that it be carried out through judicial channels, with full legal guarantees, and not as a political or symbolic measure.

Violation of sovereignty is accepted in treaties signed with Peru and Venezuela, whose troops are authorized to enter Colombian territory in the fight against the drug trade and its guerrillas. Sovereignty is also violated in the authorization granted by the U.S. Department of Justice to the FBI for the kidnapping of fugitives, without the consent of the countries where they may be, for violation of air space, which has occurred several times, and for the threat to shoot down all planes suspected of transporting drugs.

Some Recommendations. Compared with consumption of other psychoactive substances, consumption of Colombian cocaine is lowest (0.25 percent). Alcohol and cigarettes make up 85.8 percent of consumers' consumption.

The most serious problems caused by cocaine, coca paste, and marijuana consumption have to do with violence caused by the illegality of those products or substances. In 1987 a kilogram of cocaine cost, on a Colombian airstrip, between US$3,600 and US$4,400. The wholesaler in Miami paid between US$17,000 and US$22,000 (a fivefold increase), but the final retail price was between US$80,000 and US$120,000 a kilogram.

This huge profit explains the violent nature of the clandestine business since, as Marx wrote, violence is directly proportional to profit. Of the 212,144 crimes registered by the national police in 1988, narcotics crimes rated fourth, with 10,081 infractions. More prevalent were simple theft or theft and assault (69,701), crimes of bodily harm (45,865), and homicides (21,100). A good portion of the homicides and bodily harm crimes are associated with drug trafficking, which was also responsible for acts of terrorism (677 incidents), fabrication and sales of weapons and ammunition (476). Of the 70,399 persons arrested for committing crimes in 1988, the number of those who had violated norms on narcotics came third, with 11,092 persons, only topped by those who caused common personal injury (13,208 persons) and simple theft (11,542). All this implies high judiciary and judiciary police costs in investigation and arrests; costs in the destruction of fields of coca (17 hectares) and marijuana (5,309 hectares), of laboratories (655), and inputs.

In order to eliminate violence in the business of psychoactive drugs, perhaps the solution would be to study legalization in order to determine, among other things, which drugs to permit and how to legalize them, and what consequences it would have on health and society. To give marijuana and cocaine the same treatment as tobacco and alcohol would bring enormous political and social advantages—a sharp lowering of the corruption, violence, and impunity levels. There would no longer be the need to destroy the *modus vivendi* of thousands of peasants and settlers, and the high profit rate on which the mafias have thrived would disappear. One could consider legalization under state monopoly for the sale of the final product, with private plantations in the case of coca. Quality control and adequate information on consumption would prevent intoxication and deaths; price controls would dissuade consumers, but prices would not be high enough to promote smuggling.

One could also consider the legalization of the plantations and free trade in marijuana, with price control, while banning basic paste and other substances adulterated with toxic or harmful substances, because the illegal nature of the market would trigger the uncontrolled sale of low-quality drugs. Extradition for conduct not typified as crime in Colombia, and extradition for common crimes, with guarantees against sentences higher than those applied in Colombia could be done away with. All pacts or bilateral or multilateral agreements on drug traffic repression could be ended and adapted to the new requirements because this would reduce confrontation levels. Crop substitution and preventive campaigns would be necessary in the fields of education and health, with warnings about the dangers of the consumption of psychoactive substances (alcohol, cocaine, etc.). Exports would be subject to prior payment of tariffs and to quality control. The cultivation and sale of cocaine would generate income for the state, money that could be used to finance media campaigns and not the heavy cost of repressive state action, as has been the case up to now.

A SYNTHESIS OF THE DRUG ISSUE IN COLOMBIA IN THE VIRGILIO BARCO VARGAS GOVERNMENT (1986–1990) AND IN THE CESAR GAVIRIA TRUJILLO GOVERNMENT (1990–   )

The Barco government foreign policy supported the contention of internationally shared responsibility established in 1990 in the Declaration of Cartagena, an attempt to overcome the difficulties caused by policies that had polarized the supply and demand participants in illegal drug trade. While the Cartagena Summit document was largely concerned with suppression and interdiction, the acknowledgment of the United States's economic and commercial responsibilities was a step forward that should have been followed up later with multilateral action and not the bilateral agreements in fact made that ignored the Cartagena Declaration's agreements for the Andean countries. Colombia felt that the acknowledgment of shared responsibility should lead to economic and commercial compensation for the high cost of repressive measures; however, United States lobbies on the majority of issues raised by Colombia, heard in Congress, influenced President

George Bush's objections to matters like the coffee agreement or trade discrimination involved.

Barco's domestic policy was to apply the U.S. pattern of suppression by declaring "war on drugs" in Colombia, but the backlash was a spate of drug-related destructive violence of nearly Lebanese scale. Moreover, Barco's policy was undermined by unofficial talks with the drug barons to negotiate the freeing of Barco's relatives and his private secretary, kidnapped by Pablo Escobar's group, and also because the policy wrongly concentrated on the Medellin Cartel. Also, the definitions of anti-drug strategy were ambiguous. At the end of Barco's term of office, they were so patchy that the alternatives against giving priority to suppression were strengthened. Finally, Barco used extradition selectively, but the disadvantages outnumbered the advantages. The practice was a serious violation of legal procedure, which invalidated it and weakened the case for its renewal by parliament.

Cesar Gaviria's government's foreign anti-drug policy was intended to establish bilateral relations with the United States that would not be decided in terms of the drug question. The two countries would cooperate in fighting drug trafficking, with both contributing to a common treatment of the problem as an issue independent of others. The new criterion was that drug trafficking in Colombia should be distinct though not divided from international trafficking, which would affect anti-drug policies. Although the international nature of the problem had been recognized, the problems varied from country to country, and the effects do not necessarily coincide. Each country must then stress the particular aspects of the drug problem which affects it. Gaviria has kept up the usual suppression of drug trafficking within the country, using substitution and eradication campaigns and interdiction.

The Colombian air force and navy have been in charge of preventing the transport of the drug. Established methods have been used to suppress money laundering, and it was proposed to "increase international cooperation to weaken the drug trafficking networks, reduce its profits, and distribute the cost incurred more fairly."[40] This last point would be made possible via the "Special Cooperation Program" already submitted to the majority of the Northern Hemisphere countries.

Gaviria had also suggested that extradition was not the chief instrument for counternarcotics. The alternative proposed was a tougher administration of justice within a permanent legal body of expert judges. The new legal norm for drug-related crime was the State of Siege Decree 2047 issued in September 1990, which stated that extradition would be waived for those who gave themselves up and confessed the crimes committed up to the date of the decree. Prison sentences would be reduced in exchange for information about accomplices. There followed a legal and military wrangle between the extraditables, their lawyers, and the government. Extradition remained a possibility in the decree for those who did not confess all their crimes. The series of kidnappings of prominent people after the decree was issued, however, was seen as pressure to "soften" its rigid terms.

The government then issued Decrees 2372 and 3030 in October and December 1990, and finally Decree 303 in January 1991, just days after the daughter of ex-president Turbay died in an attempt by the National Police to free her from her kidnappers who were extraditables.

The traditional polarization of the executive power and the drug traffickers was altered when the National Constituent Assembly (ANC) met and established new legal and political definitions for the drug conflict. Non-extradition was made a constitutional norm, and the legal way was clear for Pablo Escobar, the notorious head of the Medellin Cartel and the most powerful Colombian drug trafficker, to surrender and validate Gaviria's autonomous handling of drug terrorism. But the state of siege and constituent decrees were not sufficient. The internal affairs of the so-called Medellin Cartel were also a drawback.

First, Pablo Escobar had lost his main followers in a war declared on the state. These included Gonzalo Rodriguez Gacha, military chief, killed in 1989; John Jairo Arias Tascon, killed in 1990; Gustavo Gaviria Rivero, Escobar's cousin and second in the hierarchy; Hernando Gaviria Gomez, killed in 1990; and David Ricardo and Armando Prisco Lopera, killed in 1991. Second, Escobar continued his customary war against the Cali drug cartel. Third, in a war against the self-defense units of Magdalena Medio, which had nearly caught him in June 1990, Escobar suffered a reverse in his military strategy. Finally, an internal purge of supposed Cali infiltrators further weakened his position.

In the United States, there were disparate reactions to Escobar's surrender. The White House declared, "The government of George Bush would prefer Pablo Escobar to be brought to the United States to be tried and will watch carefully to see if he receives due punishment in Colombia."[41] Another view was voiced by U.S. Congressman Charles Rangel (Democrat) "in prohibiting extradition, Colombia has not reneged on its commitment to put an end to the drug plague, but quite the opposite."[42]

Washington had the following expectations for Colombia:

1.   It noted the sentences given to Escobar and those others who surrendered from the Medellin Cartel, bearing in mind the penalties received by the drug traffickers convicted in the United States; Matta Ballesteros was given three life sentences and Carlos Lehder life imprisonment plus 135 years.

   The United States assumed the right to try drug traffickers who had committed drug-related crimes in the United States on their own soil. Problems can be foreseen if Colombia cannot find sufficient evidence to try the traffickers in Colombia.[43]

2. Washington was watching interdiction in Colombia. Current results favored autonomous action: Colombia had interdicted 80 percent of cocaine seized worldwide and demolished 85 percent of all laboratories.[44]

3. Now that the so-called Medellin Cartel had been disbanded, Washington was pressing for action against the Cali Cartel, which, according to press reports quoting the DEA, controls 70 percent of the cocaine brought into the United States and 90 percent of drugs sold in Europe as well as the entire market in Eastern Europe and Japan,[45] and which has formed a network with the Sicilian mafia who control heroin distribution in Europe.[46] The demand for heroin is felt in Colombia. In only three months, 2000 hectares of poppy have been eradicated.

Even this record, however, is negligible compared with DEA estimates of cocaine production in South America: in 1988 361 metric tons were produced; in 1989, 695 tons; and in 1990, 900 tons.[47] It is likely then that there is to be a major increase in military aid. This is evident in the projection in Table 4.

The 1991 CICAD Inter-American Commission on Policy Against Drug Trafficking and Drug Abuse states, "The 1992 U.S. federal budget allocates 70 percent of its funds to supply reduction programs . . . and only 30 percent to demand reduction programs." This stress on suppression forms part of the four main objectives of the Andean Anti-drug Strategy:[48]

1. concerted action and bilateral assistance to strengthen political will and capacity in Peru, Bolivia, and Colombia to attack cocaine traffic;

2. equipment, training, and cooperation for the police and military forces as part of an integrated strategy for fighting drugs (particular training to be given where the traffickers and insurgents have joint forces);

Table 4
Anti-Drug Military Aid for Colombia from the United States (in $US millions)

Years			
1989	1990	1991	1992 (required)
73.1	93.2	32.5	60.3

Source: Report of the House Foreign Affairs Committee on the International Cooperations Act of 1991 (4 June 1991).

3. improved links between the police and military, for better law enforcement, to stop money from the traffic changing hands, and to seize drugs on their way to the United States; and

4. economic aid to compensate the economic problems caused by counternarcotics programs.

Drugs are the major issue in the New International Order drafted by U.S. Defense Secretary, Dick Cheney and General Colin Powell, Chairman of the Joint Chiefs of Staff, early in 1991. The drug problem in the Andean region is presented as a regional conflict and as such is part of the U.S. security project as one of the issues emerging after the cold war.[49] One main reason for the military involvement in counternarcotics is the supposed relations between traffickers and guerrillas, which makes the problem not so much one of law enforcement as one where local and central government authority is displaced and links are forged with insurgent groups over vast areas.[50] This is an obstacle to the balanced and interdependent treatment of the problem between the United States and the Andean area.

Rather than compensate for the problems arising from military anti-drug strategies, economic aid should strengthen the Andean countries' autonomy in decisions and not leave them in a position where aid is given or withheld according to performance on the drug issue.

The United States did not accept that in the investment and trade framework agreements of the Initiative for the Americas Colombia should incorporate the best nontraditional exports that create employment in the country—textiles, garments, and leather goods. The United States also has the power to revoke trade agreements made for the Andean Initiative should they threaten U.S. interests. The United States has broken the U.S.-Colombian Coffee Agreement, has not renewed the sugar quota system, has raised tariffs on flowers, and has further impeded Colombian exports. All of these actions impede autonomous growth in Colombia and encourage the growth of the violence that appears where there is economic uncertainty.

We appeal to the need for an ethical foundation to relations between Colombia and the United States. North-South relations should be fairly balanced.

NOTES

1. UN Special Commission, Bruntland Report, in "Our Common Future." Oxford University Press, 1987.

2. Martin Lipset Seymour and Earl Raab, *La politica de la sinrazón* (Mexico: FCE, 1981), 85.

3. Ibid., 86.

4. Luis Maira, *¿Una nueva era de hegemonía norteamericana?* (Buenos Aires: Grupo Editor Latinoamericano, 1986), 25.

5. Ibid., 26.

6. Daniel Bell, "Revaloración del excepcionalismo norteamericano: El papel de la sociedad civil," *Facetas*, no. 87 (I/90), Washington, 10.

7. Ibid., 11.

8. Bruce Michael Bagley, "The New Hundred Years War? U.S. National Security and the War on Drugs in Latin America," *Journal of Interamerican Studies and World Affairs* 30, no. 1 (Spring 1988): 168.

9. Sol M. Linowitz, "Latin America, the President's Agenda," *Foreign Affairs* 67, no. 2 (Winter 1988/89): 56.

10. Ed Magnuson, "More and More, a Real War," *Time*, 22 January 1990.

11. Ana María Ezcurra, "La estrategia de seguridad post-Reagan en EE.UU." *Cuadernos IDEAS* (Buenos Aires: Instituto de Estudios y Acción Social, 1989).

12. Christian de Brie, "Market Law Imposed on Illicit Cultures," *Le Monde Diplomatique* (October 1989, Paris): 16–17.

13. This information is what is gathered from newspaper publications on the subject in the United States especially in Miami. Cf. Paul Eddy, Hugo Sabogal, and Sara Walden, *The Cocaine Wars* (New York: Bantam Books, 1988).

14. Total estimated production before transport and interdiction:

Year	Tons
1980	175
1981	180
1982	187
1983	240
1984	165
1985	206
1986	267
1987	317

Sources: Mauricio Reina, "Economía política y estrategia antidrogas: ¿Un esfuerzo fallido?" *Colombia Internacional*, no. 8 (Bogotá: Universidad de los Andes, October-December 1989), and Ethan Nadelmann, "Latinoamerica: Economía política del comercio de cocaína" ("Latin America: Economic Policy of the Cocaine Trade"), *Texto y Contexto*, no. 9 (Bogotá: Universidad de los Andes, December 1986). The above figures would seem to imply that the DEA is systematically understating effective levels of consumption in the United States.

15. Nadelmann, "Latin America: Economic Policy of the Cocaine Trade."

16. Bruce Michael Bagley, "Colombia's War on Drugs," Paper presented to the Congress of the Latin American Association, Miami, December 1989.

17. Hernando Gómez Buendía, Libardo Sarmiento Anzola, and Carlos Moreno Ospina, *Violencia, narcotráfico y producción agropecuaria en Colombia* (Violence, Drug Trafficking and Agricultural Production in Colombia) (Bogotá: Instituto de Estudios Liberales, 1989).

18. Luis Lorente, "La ganadería bovina en Colombia" ("Cattle Farming in Colombia"), in Absalón Machado, ed., *Problemas agrarios colombianos* (Colombian Agrarian Problems) (Bogotá: Siglo XXI Editores, 1986), 355.

19. Corporación de Estudios Ganaderos y Agrícolas (CEGA) *Coyuntura Agropecuaria* (Bogotá: Publicaciones Banganadero, December 1989).

20. Oscar Borrero, "La finca raiz y la economía subterránea" ("The Farm and the Underworld Economy"), Bogotá: CAMACOL, Seminario "Economía ilegal, café y construcción" ("Illegal Economy, Coffee and Construction") (8 November 1989).

21. Hernando José Gómez, "La economía ilegal en Colombia: Tamaño, evolución, características e impacto económico" ("The Illegal Economy in Colombia: Size, Evolution, Characteristics and Economic Impact"), *Coyuntura económica* (Bogotá: Fedesarrollo, September 1988).

22. Quoted by José Fernández López, in "Lunes Económico" in *El Tiempo*. Bogotá, 1989.

23. *El Tiempo*, 20 August 1983, 1A, 9A.

24. *El Tiempo*, 6 May 1980, 15A.

25. *El Tiempo*, 15 June 1981, 8B.

26. *El Tiempo*, 6 October 1982, 9B.

27. *El Espectador*, 22 November 1987, C14.

28. *El Espectador*, 12 March 1979. Extract from *Paris Match*, A3.

29. "The Guajiro problem in a cultural notion of death, a custom related to revenge, and a consequence of the power conferred by easy money." Gustavo Alvarez Gardeazabal, in *El Colombiano*, 9 July 1980, 5A.

30. Mario Arango and Jorge Child, *Coca-Coca: Historia, manejo político y mafia de la cocaína* (Coca-Coca: History, Political Handling and the Mafia of Cocaine) (Madrid: Ediciones Dos Mundos, 1986), 226.

31. *El Espectador*, 29 June 1983, 6E.

32. Cf. the June and August 1983 press campaign.

33. Daniel Samper Pizano, "Los afanados corleones criollos" ("The Determined Creole Corleones"), *El Tiempo*, 7 July 1983, 5A.

34. Juan Mayor, *El País*, 24 October 1988. Madrid. Quoted in *Nueva Sociedad*, 1989.

35. Cf. Luis Suárez Salazar, "Conflictos sociales y políticos generados por la droga," in *Nueva Sociedad*, no. 102 (July-August 1989).

36. Germán Palacio and Fernando Rojas, "Empresarios de la cocaína, para-institucionalidad y flexibilidad del régimen político colombiano," *La irrupción del paraestado* (Bogotá: Instituto Latinoamericano de Servicios Legales Alternativos (ILSA) y Centro de Estudios de la Realidad Colombiana (CEREC)), 6–7.

37. José Eduardo Faria, *Direito e Justiça* (Sao Paolo: Editora Atica, 1989), 5. Free translation.

38. Germán Palacio and Fernando Rojas, *Administración de justicia, los jueces y la crisis institucional en Colombia* (Bogota: ILSA, 1990).

39. Quoted in "Hacia una concepción latinoamericana sobre el tráfico ilícito de drogas" (Toward a Latin American Concept of Illegal Drug Trafficking) (Bogotá: Corte Suprema de Justicia, Sala Penal, Fondo de Publicaciones del Senado, 1987), 86.

40. Ibid., 34.

41. *El Tiempo*, 20 June 1991.

42. *El Tiempo*, 29 June 1991.

43. Political Constitution of Colombia, Article 35.

44. Juan G. Tokalian, in Ciro Krathausen and Luis F. Jaramillo, *Cocaine & Co* (Bogotá: Third World, 1991).

45. "Cocaine Inc., The New Drug Kings," *Time*, 1 July 1991, and "Europe's New Plague," *Time*, 1 April 1991.

46. *Newsweek*, 14 October 1991.

47. "Meanwhile, What About the Drug War," *Washington Post*, 24 February 1991.
48. Andean Antidrug Efforts: a report to the Congress (no more data).
49. *Newsweek*, 7 October 1991.
50. Andean Antidrug Efforts.

BIBLIOGRAPHY

Arango, Mario, and Jorge Child. *Coca-coca: Historia, manejo político y mafia de la cocaína*. Madrid: Ediciones Dos Mundos, 1986.

Bagley, Bruce Michael. "The New Hundred Years War? U.S. National Security and the War on Drugs in Latin America." In *Journal of Interamerican Studies and World Affairs* 30, no. 1 (Spring, 1988).

———. "Colombia's War on Drugs." Paper presented to the Congress of the Latin American Association, Miami, December 1989.

Bell, Daniel. "Revaloración del 'excepcionalismo norteamericano': El papel de la sociedad civil." *Facetas*, no. 87 (I/90), Washington.

Borrero, Oscar. "La finca raíz y la economía subterránea." Bogota: CAMACOL, Seminario "Economía legal, café y construcción." 8 November 1989.

Corporación de Estudios Ganaderos y Agrícolas (CEGA). *Coyuntura Agropecuaria*. Bogota: Publicaciones Banganadero, December 1989.

De Brie, Christian. "Market Law Imposed on Illicit Cultures." *Le Monde Diplomatique*. Paris, October 1989.

Departamento Administrativo de Seguridad (DAS). "Organización de sicarios y narcotraficantes en el Magdalena Medio." 20 July 1988. (Confidential Report).

———. "Las masacres de Urabá." 1988. (Confidential Report).

———. "Balance de la gestión oficial contra los grupos de sicarios y el narcotráfico." 1 September 1989. (Confidential Report).

Eddy, Paul, Hugo Sabogal, and Sara Walden. *The Cocaine Wars*. New York: Bantam Books, 1988.

Ezcurra, Ana María. "La estrategia de seguridad post-Reagan en EE.UU." *Cuadernos IDEAS*. Buenos Aires: Instituto de Estudios y Acción Social, 1989.

Faria, José Eduardo. *Direito e Justiça*. Sao Paolo: Editora Atica, 1989.

Fondo de Publicaciones del Senado. "Hacia una concepción latinoamericana sobre el tráfico ilícito de drogas." Bogotá: Corte Suprema de Justicia, Sala Penal, 1987.

Gómez, Hernando José. "La economía ilegal en Colombia: Tamaño, evolución, características e impacto económico." *Coyuntura económica*. Bogotá: Fedesarrollo, September 1988.

Gómez Buendía, Hernando, Libardo Sarmiento Anzola, and Carlos Moreno Ospina. *Violencia, narcotráfico y producción agropecuaria en Colombia*. Bogotá: Instituto de Estudios Liberales, 1989.

Linowitz, Sol M. "Latin America, the President's Agenda." *Foreign Affairs* 67, no. 2 (Winter 1988/89).

Lorente, Luis. "La ganadería bovina en Colombia." In Absalón Machado, ed., *Problemas agrarios colombianos*. Bogotá: Siglo XXI Editores, 1986.

Maira, Luis. *¿Una nueva era de hegemonía norteamericana?* Buenos Aires: Grupo Editor Latinoamericano, 1986.

Ministerio de Defensa Nacional. Informes al Congreso Nacional (Reports to Congress). 1987–88 and 1988–89.

Nadelmann, Ethan. "Latinoamérica: Economía política del comercio de cocaína." *Texto y Contexto*, no. 9. Bogotá: Universidad de los Andes. December 1986.

Palacio, Germán, and Fernando Rojas. "Empresarios de la cocaína, parainstitucionalidad y flexibilidad del régimen político colombiano: Narcotráfico y contrainsurgencia." *La irrupción del paraestado*. Bogotá: Instituto Latinoamericano de Servicios Legales Alternativos (ILSA) y Centro de Estudios de la Realidad Colombiana (CEREC).

———. *Administración de justicia, los jueces y la crisis institucional en Colombia*. Bogotá: ILSA, 1990.

Policia Nacional de Colombia. "Estadística de criminalidad." 1988.

Presidencia de la República. "Estrategia nacional contra la violencia." Bogotá, May 1991.

Reina, Mauricio. "Economía política y estrategia antidrogas: ¿Un esfuerzo fallido?" *Colombia Internacional*, no. 8. Bogotá: Universidad de los Andes, October-December 1989.

Seymour, Martin Lipset, and Earl Raab. *La política de la sinrazón*. Mexico: FCE, 1981.

Suárez Salazar, Luis. "Conflictos sociales y políticos generados por la droga." *Nueva Sociedad*, no. 102. Caracas: Editorial Nueva Sociedad, July-August 1989.

3

The Illicit Drug Trade in Peru

CHEMICAL AND MEDICAL ASPECTS OF COCAINE

Cocaine is an alkaloid extracted from the leaves of the coca plant (at least two species of *Erythroxilum*). The process of extraction is based on the fact that cocaine changes its solubility according to the degree of acidity of the solvent. As a salt (sulphate or hydrochloride), it is soluble in water. In its basic form, cocaine is soluble in oils and organic solvents such as benzene, kerosene, and acetone, but if an acid is added, it becomes a salt, which loses its solubility and precipitates, then being soluble in water. If an alkali is added, cocaine precipitates in the water, once again becoming soluble in oils and organic solvents.

For extraction, the dry leaf is moistened with carbonated water (to neutralize the acid) and then dried and soaked in kerosene to extract the alkaloid. Then it is precipitated with sulphuric acid, forming cocaine sulphate, which is dissolved in water. It is reprecipitated with soda, lime, or ammonia, the impure basic alkaloid then remaining as a whitish mass: the so-called basic cocaine paste (PBC). If potassium permanganate is used to oxidize and separate impurities, the washed basic paste is obtained. This paste is dissolved in ether or acetone, treated with hydrochloric acid, and made to crystallize as cocaine hydrochloride. The excess ether or acetone evaporates.

The cocaine hydrochloride may again be dissolved in water, precipitated with ammonia, and redissolved in ether. Evaporation of the ether leaves the alkaloid free as a base, which is used for smoking. If the precipitation is carried out with carbonates and the filtrate then dried, the result is crack.

The most commonly used solvents are kerosene, which may be replaced by gasoline, benzene, or oils. To prepare the hydrochloride, a volatile solvent—ether or acetone, for instance—is considered preferable. The most commonly used acids are sulphuric acid or any other acid, hydrochloric acid being preferred; hydrochloric acid is used to prepare the hydrochloride. To precipitate the alkaloid, carbonates (sodium, potassium, or calcium carbonate), sodium hydroxide (caustic soda), unslaked lime (calcium oxide), and ammonia potassium permanganate are used to oxidize the impurities.

Because cocaine production is illegal (except for the small amount for pharmaceutical use), figures on the areas cultivated and the volume of inputs used in transformation and its processes are inexact. Almost all published information is distorted since it was generally gathered by people who were unfamiliar with the chemical operations involved and unable to interpret them. The figures that follow are only "probable" or approximate with an order of magnitude of error of at least 2, but the figures do give an idea of the size of the problem. Such data are the most reliable available.

The Coca Leaf and Its Cultivation

The varieties of coca leaf in Peru (lambran, mollecoca, fusiform, ovoid, and ipadú) are grown on the eastern slopes of the Andes, at altitudes from 3,000 meters above sea level and below. In general, the lower the altitude, the lower the alkaloid content, ranging from 1.2 percent to 0.25 percent in the ipadu coca shrub of the Amazon. There is no reliable estimate as to the extent of the areas producing coca. Estimates vary from 150,000 to 320,000 hectares.

The coca leaf yield per hectare has been estimated in very different ways. Confusion is greater because the estimates rarely indicate whether it is the fresh coca leaf or the dry one (the weight difference is 40 percent), or whether the figures are per harvest or per year, since harvesting takes place three or four times a year. On the high side, the estimates for dry leaves ran to 2,400 kilograms per hectare per year in the Alto Huallaga (Marcelo); 2,200 kilograms per hectare per year for La Convención in a well-controlled study (Bues). Average figures are given as 900 to 1,300 kilograms per hectare per year (Briceno and Martinez). The best data on record for Peru are those of the old Estanco de la Coca (State Coca Leaf Monopoly) for the 1960s, with an average of 600 to 620 kilograms per hectare per year with variations of 300 to 1,400 kilograms per hectare, depending on the area. Peru's annual production could thus run anywhere between 45,000 and 448,000 tons annually. For the purpose of the following estimates, a figure of 200,000 tons annually will be taken.[1]

Cultivation of coca leaf follows three different patterns:

1. Traditional cultivation: practiced for many years by well-established campesinos making optimum use of irrigation and preventing erosion. Most of the harvest is sold to ENACO, The Empresa Nacional de la Coca (National Coca Leaf Enterprise), for legal trade.
2. Cultivation by well-established campesinos: These are farmers who usually own the land. The farmers grow crops suitable for the area, but a small area is used for coca leaf production as a way of ensuring cash and credit. The harder a farmer finds it to sell his ordinary crops, the greater the amount of his land used to cultivate the coca leaf. In general, the farmers use appropriate farming methods.
3. Uncontrolled cultivation: Some migrant farmers do not attempt to farm the land permanently. They clear the area, sow the plant, and use large amounts of defoliants and insecticides, with no thought for the soil, readily leaving behind their plots. It is they who are mainly responsible for deforestation and ecological damage to the upper jungle of the Amazon, as well as for the extensive illicit cultivation of the coca leaf.

Other Chemical Substances Involved

Kerosene is used to dissolve the alkaloid in its basic form; it is used in the proportion of 1 to 25. The clandestine laboratories employ 200 to 400 liters of kerosene for every 250 pounds of coca leaf. Kerosene may be reused by neutralizing the acid. Estimated annual consumption of kerosene in this activity must be at least 50,000 cubic meters, but in all probability it is three times more.

Sulphuric acid is used to precipitate the alkaloid dissolved in the kerosene, forming a sulphate salt. It cannot be re-used and must be discarded as sodium, calcium, or ammonium salt. The minimum theoretical amount necessary is one gram of acid to three of alkaloid in a controlled laboratory process. Under field conditions, one liter of concentrated acid is needed to precipitate the alkaloid extracted from 250 pounds of coca leaves, giving a total of 1,800 metric tons of concentrated sulphuric acid a year. For the washed basic paste, a greater amount of acid is used, which could bring the figure up to about 2,500 metric tons annually.

Alkaline substances are used in the first stage of the transformation process in order for the cocaine contained in the leaves to be turned into free base. The cocaine hydrochloride is subsequently extracted with kerosene. Alkaline substances are used afterwards to precipitate the alkaloid dissolved in water when it is in its salt form. A typical process requires 26 kilograms of potassium carbonate for 250 pounds of dry leaves, which would represent about 50,000 metric tons of potassium carbonate annually for the first stage. The final stage requires about 1,800 metric tons of ammonia or 5,400 metric tons of unslaked lime a year.

About 1,800 metric tons of potassium permanganate are also used annually to remove the high proportion of cinamoil cocaine. The presence of cinamoil cocaine allows an analyst to detect which transformation process has been used.

This chemical transformation process permits the extraction of about 7 kilograms of the basic cocaine paste (PBC) from each metric ton of dry leaves, giving an annual production of about 1,400 metric tons of PBC.

The drug produced along the eastern slopes of the Peruvian Andes goes to different destinations. Part goes by air to Colombia. Another part goes by river to Brazil, and the rest goes to the Peruvian coast for local consumption, final processing, and distribution to other countries. All reports agree that the main destination is Colombia by air in light planes that carry half a ton each flight.

FACTORS OF DRUG DEPENDENCE

Drug dependence does not occur in all individuals, which has led to a classification of different ways a drug is used: occasional and recreational and compulsive users. The term *compulsive* is used when there is addiction, but this classification is misleading. What one individual may consider recreational may seem manifestly pathological to an outside observer.

A number of factors lead an individual to try a drug. Other factors lead to compulsive use. In essence, the capacity of a drug to produce addiction is of prime importance, affecting the rapidity and intensity with which addiction can appear. The factors leading to addiction are (1) individual physical factors, (2) psychological factors, and (3) environmental factors, such as the influence of family, peers, and society in general.

First, drug dependence has been attributed to genetic causes, as is the case with alcohol. In the case of cocaine, a genetic cause has recently been described that affects the lithium transport rate. In these and other cases, basic psychiatric disturbances such as manic-depressive psychoses, major depression, and dysthymic depression may occur.

Second, there is frequently a relative inability of a drug user to cope with the environment. This inability may be expressed in two important ways: through difficulty in handling feelings and emotions, leading to conduct of avoidance or escape and eventually to drug use; or through lack of self-control, with a person being unable to strive for even short-term goals due to a need for immediate satisfactions. Once this habit starts, it is followed by a loss of a person's already very limited self-esteem.

Third, the influences of family, peers, and society are critical. It is certainly clear that inadequate family relationships produce maladjustments predisposing someone to drug use or triggering the habit. "Inadequate" family relationships should be understood not only as difficulties with parents or between parents, but also experiences with improper rewards and punishments, troubles in giving and withdrawing affection, and the failure to achieve self-control or to develop self-esteem. In many cases, the breakup of a family and the innumerable problems that result affect a person's emotional stability and predispose him or her to seek out and abuse drugs.

It is also said that an addict becomes a member of a peer group that has its own language, secret codes, and manipulative, often criminal behavior. This group suffers a generalized psychopathy, loss of values, and estrangement from social norms. The person gradually changes his/her circle of friends, spending more time with those belonging to the "drug culture" and less with non-addicts. Friendships deteriorate. Once a group of addicts has been formed, it is very difficult to leave. It may be attractive to those who, having had an inadequate family relationship or sentimental problems, find escape from their problems.

In Peru a number of social characteristics are conducive to sustained use of drugs. Since social drugs (alcohol and tobacco) are used very liberally, it is customary and desirable to use psychotropic drugs as an escape, making inhaling something quite normal. Hence economic decline, poverty, lack of opportunities, and the presence of diverse ethnic and cultural groups, all lead to the loss of values, frustration, violence, and corruption that both foster favorable conditions for drug trafficking and contribute to an individual maladjustment that may find a form of escape in the use of drugs.

Cocaine has many effects on the body, and texts on pharmacology classify the drug in several ways:

- It is a local anesthetic, one of the first ever used and one of the most potent, and although still employed, its use is limited, due to the dangers involved;
- It reinforces physiological and pharmacological stimulation of the sympathetic nervous system;
- It acts strongly on the central nervous system, stimulating some centers and inhibiting others, and producing psychic stimulation; and
- At present, its main effect is its capacity to produce pronounced dependence, making it probably the most difficult to treat of all known drug addictions.

Cocaine's capacity to produce psychic stimulation and addiction depends on the speed with which its concentration increases in the central nervous system, and this speed varies with the speed of absorption into the body. Hence cocaine's effects are measured and not addictive when consumed as coca-leaf tea. During coca-leaf chewing (*acullico*), the effect is moderate and addiction occurs after a long period and large doses. Finally, when consumed as the hydrochloride applied to the mucous membrane, intense effects may be produced, resulting in addiction when used repeatedly and in large doses.

Cocaine base may be smoked in special pipes or with tobacco or marijuana cigarettes. The absorption and addiction rate is very high when smoked. At the beginning of the 1970s, the basic paste began to be smoked in Peru, which was consumed as *basuco* in Colombia and as free base in the United States, producing severe addiction that led to the description of a new and rapidly developing syndrome, one of great severity and difficult treatment. Cocaine addiction rapidly extended throughout South America and in the form of crack, it did the same in the United States from the mid-eighties onwards.

The use of cocaine taken in any form produces a stimulating psychic effect, usually euphoria, a sensation of well-being, alertness, superiority, and the capacity to feel and do extraordinary things. Hunger, fatigue, and alcoholic torpor disappear. The intensity and duration of this effect depend on the way cocaine is taken. The euphoria, or "high," is followed by a proportionate dysphoric stage of depression and malaise. Repeated use of the drug gradually changes the patterns of sensation: the euphoria becomes shorter and the dysphoria (depression) more accentuated. A craving that progressively subjugates the interests of the individual develops until the only desire is to take the drug. A cocaine user begins to lie and swindle and is, in general, capable of committing any crime in order to continue the new life-style. With the psychopathological tendencies come new symptoms that depend not so much on the drug as on the new behavior patterns: loss of weight, personal neglect, infections, general decline, abandonment of studies or job, and impotence. Often the use of the drug leads to hallucinations and grave psychosis or death due to heart attacks or crimes associated with the illicit drug trade. Treatment is extremely difficult and becomes more so the longer the addiction has existed. The illness does not affect the addict alone. The family, too, is directly affected.

Cocaine consumption was not a public health problem in Peru until the 1970s. Up to that time, the drug was consumed as the hydrochloride, inhaled nasally in small amounts by people obliged to work at night, to drink alcohol for reasons of their work, or as a status symbol by high society. The seventies brought more intensive cocaine use through sniffing combined with other drug habits; groups of young people who had been accustomed to other drugs such as marijuana and LSD used higher doses each time. At the same time, people began to smoke the basic paste, producing case histories as had never before been seen in Peru of extreme severity and very resistant to therapy.

The number of admissions to psychiatric hospitals increased considerably. For example, the Hermilio Valdizan Psychiatric Hospital records that between 1977 and 1981, 602 patients were admitted with cocaine related problems, constituting 14 percent of all patients. No updated figures are available for the entire country.

The most reliable epidemiological surveys revealed that about 4 percent of people between 12 and 45 years of age living in cities of more than 25,000 inhabitants have taken cocaine at some time. Consumption rose to nearly 8 percent among men, and up to 14 percent among men from 20 to 29 years of age. The problems arising from drug use were reflected in police statistics, which revealed a rapid increase in drug consumption. In 1983, there were 416 cases and police reports involving cocaine-paste consumers. By 1987, the number had risen to 1,699 and is still growing.[2]

COCA AND THE PERUVIAN ECONOMY

Coca has always been part and parcel of Peruvian life and, above all, of Peru's economy. Yet its importance has varied enormously throughout the country's history. Today, with Peruvian society practically falling apart, coca looms larger than ever and inquiries into its economic impact become especially relevant.

The use of the coca leaf in Peru dates back to prehistoric times, as we know from both ample archeological evidence and frequent references in the chronicles written under the early viceroys recording Inca and pre-Inca traditions and customs. As Roberto Lerner has stated, the use of the coca leaf by the inhabitants of the Andes in those days, and even today,

goes beyond the possible stimulating effects that help human beings adapt to basically hostile environments. Unquestionably, it has a deep social significance and forms part of the Andean inhabitant's vision of the cosmos. [Although the number of coca leaf chewers has been dropping, above all in the last ten years, some two million people still chew it. We should not lose sight of the fact that coca leaf] is a substance with a legitimate role to play in a particular culture. It is therefore not a question of studying its effects on health in isolation from that cultural context.[3]

With the arrival of the Spaniards, the areas planted with coca increased, and use of the leaf almost certainly became more widespread. The attitude of the newcomers toward it was about as ambiguous as most people's attitudes today. On the one hand, the Spaniards considered the traditional use of coca to be a form of resistance against the onslaught of Spanish culture. On the other hand, they were quick to spot its trading value. From 1543 onwards, the rulers of Peru issued a series of laws and regulations banning, protecting, or regulating the sowing and use of the coca shrub. In the process, more and more importance was attached to the economic aspects of coca.

The "international" use of coca dates back to the end of the nineteenth century, when chemists isolated the cocaine in it and began to use it as an anaesthetic. It was then that Peruvian exports of the coca leaf began. The boom period occurred in the first ten years of this century, with Peru managing at one point to export 1,331 metric tons a year. Then came a period of decline—although exports continued—first due to competition from other countries and later because, except for restricted and monitored uses, cocaine was declared illegal.

Nevertheless coca growing, processing, and exporting became increasingly important in the second half of this century, finally reaching crisis point. This growth coincided with mass migration from the countryside to cities, which resulted in improved health services, which, in turn, resulted in a dramatic population boom starting in the 1950s. Although the process has its positive side—improved education, for example—the swift changes in the population structure resulted in the migrants losing their old social order without becoming completely integrated within the "Western" patterns of urban society. In turn, the public administration systems were overwhelmed; they became, for instance, increasingly incapable of offering even essential services, security, or employment:

This has caused vast sectors of the population to develop survival strategies beyond the confines of formal society. There is a general mistrust of the organizations and institutions entrusted with law enforcement and administration of justice. It seems that two phenomena arose as a response to the situation. On the one hand, movements catering to people's strong sense of belonging and vital urge . . . and, on the other, a middle class search for sources of employment, wealth, and social legitimacy, among them everything connected with the cocaine industry.[4]

It was in this social setting that the illicit drug trade took off in Peru. In the mid-seventies, there was a dramatic increase in world demand for cocaine, sparking off an enormous expansion of illicit coca growing in Peru, above all in new areas such as the Upper Huallaga. And so it was that the scourge of drug trafficking appeared in Peru with the corruption produced by the tremendous profits previously seen in the nations where the drug was consumed. The entire process was accelerated by the extraordinary profits involved compared to the limited and uncertain profits from other crops and their dependence on insufficient and inefficient official credit and marketing systems.

Sudden wealth brought regional bonanzas and accelerated migration, disorderly growth, and disregard of the central government by local leaders.

As a clandestine productive activity, drug trafficking generated a completely anarchic form of economic growth and, above all, one impossible to sustain over the long term. For example, in the Upper Huallaga, most towns have banks and sophisticated communications and entertainment services. The inhabitants of these areas have had rapid access to modern life-styles and advanced technology, arousing in them radically new expectations and aspirations. In violent contrast, however, other towns lack basic public services such as drinking water, sewerage, schools, and adequate police protection. Health services are rudimentary. The streets are unpaved, and there is an almost complete absence of cultural activities. Savings generated by the drug trade are not invested in the area except for further illegal activities, so that development of a kind that is integrated with the rest of the nation becomes impossible.

The influence of coca nevertheless stains the entire nation and distorts its economy. Compare, for instance, the value of the basic cocaine paste produced in 1988 (about US$1,900 million, as we shall see), with the value of total legal exports of goods for that year (which amounted to US$2,690 million). In other words, cocaine paste exports were equivalent to 70 percent of the total. Faced with this situation, the Peruvian government and the country's ruling class have adopted an ambiguous and even contradictory attitude. On the one hand, they authorize extremely severe, repressive legal measures with police raids on clandestine laboratories, the arrest of drug smugglers, and some timid eradication and crop substitution efforts. At the same time, a lax attitude is taken toward the foreign exchange generated by the drug trade. Its "contribution" to the balance of payments is defended despite the demonstrable damage to legal exports and the (less protected) local market by the illicit influx of dollars. The foreign exchange resulting from drug trafficking also distorts figures, conceals realities and, worse still, is conducive to economic policies that result in grave damage to the nation.

A study of the garment industry in Colombia in 1981 showed investment, maximum output capacity, growth of domestic demand, and output figures that were not even remotely consistent with the official export volumes reported. Many exporting firms then were impossible to find. As for the "concealing of reality," although Peru prosecutes drug money laundering, the abundant foreign exchange in the informal money market indicates toleration with the Central Reserve Bank itself indirectly acquiring "narco-dollars." However, this abundance of dollars produced at extremely low cost compared to lawful alternatives depresses the free market–exchange rate and the official exchange rates, reducing the profitability of other exports and leaving agriculture and local industry seriously unprotected. The damage produced is immense, and it is a decisive factor in Peru's economic crisis in the 1970s and 1980s. In addition, in order to appropriate the much-needed foreign exchange generated by the drug trade, the Central Reserve Bank has to buy foreign currency surpluses on the market. However, since there are no surpluses in the treasury to finance such purchases, the Central Bank issues unbacked currency and thereby fuels inflation. Thus, both monetary and exchange-rate policies suffer from the increasing role of drug dollars in the Peruvian economy.

Drug smuggling has an even more pernicious effect on a country's development and its social values. To establish a pattern of self-sustaining growth requires hard work, accumulation of savings, and the application of those savings to investment and capital formation so that tomorrow's labors may yield more wealth with less effort. But the drug trade does the opposite: it produces instantaneous profit, makes savings difficult, and distorts investment patterns. In general, it creates expectations of high returns over the short term with little effort. The same is expected of other less profitable activities with the result that such activities are postponed or rejected. A bias is created in favor of consumption and speculation and against investment in physical or financial capital or in culture and education.

Immediate steps must be taken to solve the economic issue of drug trafficking. Unfortunately, results can be obtained only over the long term. There must be a consistent strategy with a transition period during which there is an alternative source of foreign exchange while new economic activity is being generated. And at the same time, the harmful effects of this moral and social scourge are to be combatted and attempts made to stabilize and pacify the country. For all this to be achieved, one prerequisite is deeper knowledge of what is to be changed.

Coca Leaf Production

There are many different estimates as to the volume of production of coca leaves. In any event, a cautious and moderate estimate would be 150,000 hectares under cultivation in 1989, which represents an average of official estimates. The upper limit would be the 320,000 hectares appearing in a Post Graduate Business Administration school (ESAN) study.

It is important to point out that the productive potential of the coca leaf is not determined by land or labor resources but by demand for the product. The greater the demand, the greater will be the replacement of legal products by the coca. More land will be made available for the same purpose. That is why there are also different estimates of the hectares that could be cultivated in Peru. In this respect, the figure of 320,000 hectares constitutes only the minimum potential area. Lastly, it is clear that the figure refers to unauthorized crops since, in addition, there were 17,174 hectares sown with the coca shrub in 1988, with production being sold to the National Coca Company

(ENACO) to be officially marketed in Peru (for traditional uses) and abroad (mainly for medical use). Of the 150,000 unauthorized hectares considered as the probable area under cultivation in 1989, about 60,000 are in the Upper Huallaga valley, making it the largest coca leaf producing area in the world. This cultivation produces an average yield of 1.8 metric tons of coca leaves per hectare per year, according to surveys made by a private business group in the Upper Huallaga area. According to Roberto Lerner, such productivity is feasible. Therefore, the total volume of coca leaves produced in 1989 would be 270,000 tons.[5]

Using a price per ton of US$2,600[6] gives a production value of unprocessed coca leaf in the order of US$700 million. This entire sum would enter the Peruvian economic system, since the coca leaf is generally paid for in local currency after the drug traffickers sell their dollars. However, it should be pointed out that production of the coca leaf involves very variable yields and, hence, the respective flow of foreign currency. The figure cited is only a good approximation and assumes that, in recent years, there have been improvements in Peruvian coca leaf cultivation techniques. Higher yields have been achieved particularly shortening the length of time needed for the coca shrub to reach maturity. The result has been more harvests per year and higher productivity per harvest.

Production of Basic Cocaine Paste (PBC)

The production of basic cocaine paste is an intermediate process required to produce cocaine. The yield from the 150,000 hectares under illegal cultivation with coca leaf would be converted into basic paste, a process entirely carried out in Peru. To estimate the total value of the basic paste, 270,000 metric tons of coca leaves have been considered, with an average conversion factor of 0.01 as indicated in the studies performed in the Upper Huallaga valley. This process gives 2,700 tons of basic paste with an average value per kilogram in 1988 of US$700, according to the same studies, giving a grand total of US$1,890 million, which is what is estimated to be the gross revenue from drug trafficking entering the Peruvian economy in 1989.

Economic Activity Level and Coca

The lawful gross domestic product of Peru for 1989 has been estimated at US$16 billion. Dividing this value by the assumed amount of foreign exchange remaining in the economy as a consequence of drug trafficking, an average of nearly 11 percent of GDP is obtained. Since this estimate does not include the clandestine economy generated by drug trafficking, its addition would round out the final figure to 11 percent, which gives a rough idea of the enormous economic and financial impact of the business.

If we consider that drug trafficking revenue becomes part of the national productive process, and if we take the input-output matrix prepared by the Instituto Nacional de Estadistica (National Statistics Institute) to estimate the imported component within the economy, it is seen that with that variable alone, that is, without considering linkages and multiplier effects, instantaneous elimination of the drug trade would cause a drop in the GDP on the order of 4 percent, a figure higher than the rate of population growth (2.6 percent) and greater than the average economic growth rate in the last thirty years (3.04 percent).

To cite a more recent effect, had there been no foreign exchange revenue from drug trafficking in 1988, the drop in GDP that year would have been 12.6 percent, rather than the 8.8 percent recorded in official statistics. On the other hand, about 600,000 people (more than 3 percent of the total population) depend directly or indirectly on coca-leaf cultivation. Major clandestine economic boosts derived from drug smuggling ought also to be taken into account, and these often take the form of business "fronts," especially in the services sector as well as in financial intermediation.

As to the local effects in the areas where there is coca-leaf production, it is obvious that the economic importance of drug trafficking is greater. These areas have become poles of attraction, particularly for the inhabitants of the most impoverished areas of the highlands. For example, in the seventies and first half of the eighties, the Upper Huallaga valley had a population growth rate of 4.2 percent, far above the national average of 2.6 percent. Furthermore, it is useful to know that 40 percent of the newcomers had lived on the coast before migrating to the high jungle.

One aspect of the state's presence and activity that is worth highlighting is that it fosters migration, above all by building roads. However, the state then nearly disappears, leaving behind infrastructure and access roads that are utilized by settlers who have abandoned the poverty of their hometowns, lured by the glitter of a region with a wealth of opportunities—chief among them, coca. Furthermore, cultivation systems tend to involve clearing the jungle and then passing on to other plots rather than re-sowing the previous one, which produces instability and great mobility, especially since there is no way to establish land tenure and ownership. In addition, without property deeds, farmers are not eligible for loans or technical assistance, which discourages producers from shifting to other crops. All this produces a vicious circle, from which drug smugglers and local chiefs, including subversive leaders who encourage and protect settlers, draw the greatest benefit.

A large majority of the settlers in these regions are full time or part time coca farmers and an increasing number are manufacturing basic cocaine paste. It is estimated that more than 60 percent of the family farmers in the Upper Huallaga plant coca. Other landowners harvest with paid labor, while living in the towns, where almost all of the industries and services support or live off drug trafficking. Thus, there is almost total dependence on coca, rendering any attempt at eradication enormously difficult.

The deciding factor is the huge difference in profits between coca and any other crop, or even any other economic activity unrelated to drug trafficking. According to the coefficients established by surveys and studies,[7] coca growers invest about US$100 million and sell their output for US$700 million. Individually, they make about US$4,000 net per hectare per year (a profit of US$600 million for 150,000 hectares cultivated). Other products, even with the advantage of credits and subsidized inputs, yielded much less in 1987: US$1,925 per hectare in the case of palm oil (after a long period of maturation); for cacao, US$975; rice, US$720; and corn, US$240 per hectare.

In the form of basic paste, coca fetches US$700 per kilogram, making it an extremely valuable cargo with respect to its weight, even profitable when flown out by chartered planes. Shipping out other products is quite different; often they involve large volumes per hectare, and few are processed. Freight costs represent a large percentage of the final price, above all when the goods must be transported huge distances by river, with inadequate port services en route, or over very poor roads before reaching the Pacific Coast and Peru's big consumer markets and ports for export shipment. It is important therefore to establish local agribusinesses to improve profit margins for other crops and solve the problem of high freight costs.

The economic significance of the coca leaf and basic cocaine paste in the producing areas can be seen in the 1980–87 period when Peru's GDP (including the coca economy) grew 15.2 percent, but that of the coca-growing departments grew more: Amazonas increased by 30.5 percent; Huanuco, 23.8 percent; and Ucayali, 33.3 percent. San Martin had a growth rate slightly higher than that of national GDP. The drug trade is clearly thriving in the coca-leaf-producing regions. During the first half of the 1980s in the Upper Huallaga, there were six main crops (rice, starchy corn, potatoes, yucca, beans, and bananas), as well as coca, that showed growth rates. From 1985 on, only the coca shrub and African palm oil increased in cultivated area. Coca has quite clearly replaced traditional crops more and more.[8]

In 1988, a period of a profound economic recession and high inflation in Peru, local currency (*inti*) deposits in the banking system fell markedly in real terms. Nationwide, they dropped 6.6 percent, but in the coca-growing departments, the drop was less (–1 percent in Huanuco), and in some cases there was even growth (1.7 percent in San Martin). This statistic gives us a first clue as to the incidence of drug trafficking in the financial and banking systems, an issue that merits further attention.

DRUG TRADE, FOREIGN EXCHANGE, AND
THE BANKING SYSTEM

In 1989, the estimated value in U.S. dollars of illegal exports of basic cocaine paste was on the order of US$1,890 million, which is equivalent to 70 percent of total legal exports that year, 98 percent of so-called traditional exports, and 159 percent of mining exports, usually considered the main source of Peru's foreign exchange. Unquestionably, then, Peru is already a "drug addict," dependent on drug money to supply vital foreign exchange. Nevertheless, today's statistics reflect not just the increase in output of basic paste but also Peru's weak export record.

Back in 1980, legal exports were worth US$3,916 million. By 1988, these had actually dropped to US$2,690 million, due to the anti-export policy bias of both the Alan Garcia Perez and Fernando Belaunde Terry governments, 1985–1990 and 1980–1985 respectively, caused to a large extent by the growth of illegal foreign exchange income. In fact, this "black market" supply tended to depress the exchange rate, thereby seriously hindering the development of legal exports. Furthermore, the lack of a sufficiently high exchange rate encouraged the entry of "cheap" imports, thus jeopardizing agriculture and industry and, consequently, further affecting the balance of payments.

If the illegal entry of foreign exchange were to decrease, the proper conditions would be created to increase exports, raise the competitiveness of domestic production, and doubtless, after a certain amount of time, improve Peru's balance of payments. As to the "destination" of those US$1,890 million—assuming it were possible to isolate them—about US$900 million "financed" capital flight and dollar hoarding by the public, according to an investigation carried out for the U.S. Agency for International Development (USAID) in Lima by Macroconsult S.A. The remaining US$1,000 million entered the economy to cover imports of goods and services, including smuggling: US$500 million through the banking system and US$500 million directly.

To gauge the impact of the gross value of basic cocaine paste on the banking system, it suffices to recall that US$1,890 million was equivalent to 98 percent of total liquidity in banks and finance corporations at the end of 1988 and equivalent to 188 percent of all local and foreign currency deposits at that time. However, the seriousness of the problem demands that the Central Reserve Bank defend the stability of the currency and administer international reserves wherever there are uncontrolled "black-market" inflows of such magnitude—a situation due more to the application of erroneous policies than to the increase of drug trafficking. Although the influx of illegal foreign exchange is high, its relative proportion to the financial system is exaggerated by Peru's huge inflation, which has led to ridiculously low levels of real terms liquidity. This is another topic well worth clearing up.

From these figures, it is clear that in 1988 the Central Reserve Bank lost control of a major part of the money supply. The bank's monetary program stalled because it catered for only a part of the huge influx of drug dollars, that is, the US$500 million gain in international assets resulting from the purchase of foreign exchange on the free market by financial institutions. On the other hand, the reduction in financial intermediation by the Central Bank, together with increased direct use of dollars instead of *intis* (once again as a consequence of hyperinflation), has led to a hoarding of foreign exchange by the public equivalent to 50 percent of total local and foreign currency deposits (the other US$500 million of the financial system).

Therefore, monetary policy and its tools (especially interest rates, legal reserve requirements, and the purchase and sale of securities) were severely limited, resulting in another way in which drug trafficking produced distortions in the Peruvian economy. Exchange-rate policy was especially affected. The Central Bank not only issued *Intis* for an equivalent of US$500 million, due to the gain in reserves resulting from the exports of drugs, but it did so at an exchange rate influenced by that very increase and, indirectly, by the other US$1,200 million used without financial intermediation.

This important mass of resources, or at least part of it, was financing both the formal and informal economy of the nation. Equally, that portion of it that entered the financial system permitted many of its institutions to balance their accounts, which had been badly hit by an inflationary and depression-oriented economy. All of these factors once again highlighted the need for a period of transition and "adjustment," should the illegal income from drugs be suppressed.

COSTS OF THE DRUG TRADE

In addition to the direct costs of repressive measures taken by the police against drug trafficking, the upkeep of those imprisoned for such crimes, and the costs of the respective administration of justice, as well as other public and private expenditures to fight and overcome this scourge, there are other social costs that are difficult to measure but are more significant. A discussion of some of these social costs follows.

Ecological Aspects

According to estimates in a study by Aramburú and Bedoya, deforestation related directly or indirectly to cultivation of the coca leaf has reached a total of 700,000 hectares in the high jungle. This has proceeded at a dizzying rate from the time of the coca leaf boom in the mid-1970s. When land is to be used for the cultivation of the coca shrub, the area must be cleared, weeded, and burned for each harvest (two to four times a year), leaving the soil prone to erosion. The fragile ecosystem, heavy rainfall, sandy-clay soils, sloping terrain, deforestation, defoliation, and so on are leading to dramatic results: at the rate that the high jungle soils are being destroyed, it will practically be desert in a few decades.[9]

Fertilizers and bioxides that are almost always inorganic are usually used intensively and without the rational controls applying to legal, regulated farming. The chemicals used in the preparation of basic cocaine paste in the so-called *pozas* (pits) are dumped into the rivers. It is estimated that in 1986 the rivers near the pits received discharges of 57 million liters of kerosene; 32 million liters of sulphuric acid; 16 metric tons of unslaked lime; 3,200 metric tons of carbides; 16,000 metric tons of toilet tissue; 6,400 liters of acetone; and a similar quantity of toluene.[10]

These products have caused the extinction of fish, crustacea, amphibia, and river bank plants. The Amazon region, of which the Peruvian upper jungle is a part, contains the greatest variety of genetic species in the world, but it is being depredated at breakneck speed. Yet the ecosystem is of utmost importance for the future economic development of Peru.

Poorly coordinated police operations use chemicals and crop eradication and substitution programs that fail to take into account all the factors at stake. Doubtless the harm done to ecological systems by these activities is not deliberate and may be a byproduct of necessary tasks, but corrective measures should certainly be feasible.

Health Aspects

The idea that drug consumption was a secondary problem of no particular importance in the so-called coca-leaf-producing nations is no longer valid in light of the most recent statistics. In effect, ready availability has resulted in a rapid increase in the demand for the drug in such countries and even in the in-transit nations. In Peru, the situation is aggravated by the fact that the most readily available form is the most dangerous one—basic cocaine paste. The last study performed by the Drug Abuse Prevention Center (CEDRO) reveals the following use patterns: alcohol, 88 percent; cigarettes, 63 percent; painkillers, 17 percent; marijuana, 6.2 percent; basic cocaine, 1.8 percent. The use of the coca leaf runs at 13.4 percent. In the case of basic cocaine paste, 98 percent of those who consume it, in the age group between twenty and forty years of age, are men. The highest prevalence rate after Lima is that of the jungle region, which lends support to the notion that availability engenders vice.

Barsallo and Gordillo indicate that there are about 600,000 occasional users of the drug in Lima and Callao, but according to other opinions, this figure appears to be extremely high.[11] Roberto Lerner[12] indicates that a conservative estimate would be 35,000 addicts for the entire country in 1987. Even so, the cost of treating such a number would be unmanageable. The most serious aspect is that each year there is a progressive increase in the number of addicts. Therefore Peruvian society faces growing direct economic costs that are generally and mistakenly not taken into account in analyzing the pros and cons of drug trafficking in the country.

The Cost of Economic Distortions

There is no doubt whatsoever that the production of basic cocaine paste and the profits from the drug trade that remain in Peru seriously distort the national economy. Some distortions are measurable, although there is still no complete study on the subject. The greatest distortion is that, due to the easy inflow at low cost of a mass of foreign exchange disproportionately high with respect to the balance of payments, governments feel tempted to pursue and finance clearly anti-export foreign exchange policies that leave the domestic market unprotected. The approximately US$1,000 million generated by the illegal export of basic cocaine paste that remained in the 1989 economy required an exchange rate that, often enough, was way below theoretical equilibrium parity for that year.

With this in mind, often enough the authorities claim that raising the exchange rate to a level approaching its theoretical parity value would "benefit" the drug traffickers who, on obtaining additional profits, would bring in fewer dollars. In truth, such a lag makes the national economy increasingly more dependent on illegal drug revenue. When, as in the past thirty years, the exchange rate is set beneath its parity level, legal exports languish. The lack of a profit margin frequently prevents exports taking place at all. No major foreign-exchange generating projects have been carried out in Peru for many years now. As a result, the volume of Peru's exports has remained low or at a standstill, making the country dependent on international prices to increase its reserves and even forcing it to resort to foreign loans, when available, beyond reasonable levels.

The other side of the coin is the damage done by imports, which is perhaps even greater. Peru's domestic market is so unprotected that in order to prevent profound recessions, governments have generally resorted to inefficient regulatory and control systems with differential rates, high and scattered subsidies, tariff rates, tax policies riddled with exemptions, and other methods of a similar ilk, in a vain attempt—since they are insufficient over the medium term—to make up for the lack of an appropriate single exchange rate. This distorts the entire economy and makes it inefficient as a whole, producing corruption, another facet of the drug trade.

The result is a lower standard of living leading to violence. For example, everyone is aware that priority should be given to farming. Not only was the average exchange rate insufficient in 1989 to provide a degree of prosperity but there was a lack of protection through prices, the rural areas receiving inefficient subsidies in the form of low–interest rates that simply limit future loans for farmers or inputs.

Competing foreign products were not subject to tariffs or the tariffs were far less than those on inputs and machinery required by farming activities. Some foreign products were even imported at "special" exchange rates below the average, following generally arbitrary, if not anarchic, multiple-rate systems. In other words, the distortions obstructing farm development reveal a very clear regressive trend with respect to income distribution. Violence and terrorism follow, reinforcing the vicious circle of falling incomes, while the country increases its dependence on food from abroad, an overall phenomenon that not even the most extreme demagogy could conceal. Nothing like this could have been sustained beyond brief periods, without the inadequate exchange rate being financed through a massive influx of illicit foreign exchange.

There is no question that the prevailing poverty has been reinforced, rather than alleviated, by the foreign exchange generated through drug trafficking. The situation also changes the behavior of entrepreneurs: they want quick profits instead of thinking in terms of investments in fixed assets, financing, and training, which, in the medium term, produce greater and surer benefits. In turn, drug trafficking generates an active and important underground economy that evades taxes and is oriented toward services and other high turnover activities with few fixed assets. Furthermore, drug trafficking also interacts with the lawful and formal economy, in the coca-producing areas characterized by a feverish activity quite out of pace with the rest of the country. Unfortunately, the ecological costs exceed the local benefits even in the presumably favored areas. Other important distortions occur in monetary and exchange rate transactions within the economic system. Undoubtedly, the volume of operations arising from the influx of drug dollars vis-à-vis monetary emission, liquidity, and reserves, seriously hampers the work of the Central Reserve Bank and generates inflation, although it must be emphasized that the negative effects result more from inadequate economic policies.

All of these economic consequences occur due to money-laundering operations, which produce economic activities whose financing basically depends on trafficking in the coca leaf and its derivatives. The businesses serving as fronts almost always belong to the commerce and service sectors, such as restaurants, travel agencies, hotels, and so on—in general, all businesses that do not require a great investment and where the money has a rapid turnover permitting easy manipulation of expenses.

Lastly, there are also businesses that although not serving as a complete front for the business, nevertheless are the means used for laundering drug-trafficking profits, as enterprises that finance an important part of their expenses using such funds, for example, banking institutions operating with foreign currency. Such organizations find it difficult not to recognize the provenance of the resources they use, although in Peru their guilt is no greater than that of their peers in the large consumer nations, where corruption in any event deals with far larger sums.

The role of monetary intermediation in the Peruvian financial system was again diminished in real terms, as of the second half of 1989, due to the crisis produced by inflation and recession. With the fall in their raw material—the currency with which they worked—greater than the drop in their operating and administrative costs, banks' normal financial income was insufficient to cover expenses. As a result, the institutions of the system sought other income. Purchase and sale of foreign currencies were among those operations most actively developed to solve profitability issues.

Foreign-exchange operations, which in Peru are almost exclusively in U.S. dollars, are carried out in different ways, the most common being the "teller's window" where the client is not required to declare the origin or the destination of the foreign money in the transaction. Then there are interme-diate variations where transactions are performed over the phone or through "authorized agents" in the *Ocoña* free market (the area where street vendors buy and sell dollars for *intis*). It is usual for the identity of the buyer to be kept secret.

Banks and finance companies generally obtain black-market dollars in amounts restricted by the Central Reserve Bank (however, from November 1988 all restrictions were lifted). For that purpose, the banks and finance companies set up operating funds directly or through agents. The average price at which these dollars are acquired is the minimum that the banks will defend to avoid exchange losses. The Central Bank operates through the financial system and buys and sells foreign exchange according to the exchange regulations set for those markets and occasionally on *Ocoña* street, mostly at a level close to that of the "free bank-exchange rate" set by the Superintendency of Banks and Insurance.

As was previously mentioned, Macroconsult S.A. estimates that in 1988 US$500 million of drug money were laundered through the Peruvian finan-cial system, with operations being concentrated in three or four banks with branches in coca-growing areas. Even though the Central Reserve Bank has been acquiring black-market foreign exchange on a daily basis since 1985, the system is basically law-abiding, since money laundering of illegally acquired dollars is not a part of the standard practice of institutions. The Dirección General de Contribuciones (Tax Office) handles information regarding the origin of capital in all real estate purchases, which makes it difficult to avoid detection in transactions involving large sums or even chattel. Despite this and the fact that corruption in Peru is not as extensive as it is in other producer and consumer nations, both money laundering and the corruption of officials, judges, and police are increasing rapidly.

THREE STAGES OF PERUVIAN DRUG TRADE LEGISLATION

Peruvian legislation related to the drug trade can be viewed in three distinct stages. The first period of illicit drug-trade legislation began on 11 March 1920 with the declaration of the Customs Code, which apparently lasted until 1946. The government was caught up with the abuses by consumers that were going on in the formal marketplace and with its attempts to regulate them. Regulations addressed only those drugs used for medication. Opium smoking was the exception, with its use being legal for a good part of this period, even though it was subsequently prohibited.

During that period, Peruvian legislation kept closely to the guidelines set by the League of Nations dealing with the illicit drug trade during the 1920s and 1930s. Products considered drugs (including salts and other derivatives) during that stage included opium (Act 4428, 26 November 1921); morphine (Act 4428); cocaine (Act 4428); heroin (Act 44268); yohimbine, incorporated into the list in 1928 but withdrawn in 1945; and sulphuric ether, also included in the 1928 list and whose medical prescription was legalized as of 1932. In 1941 controls covering poppy cultivation and its use were established.

The main areas covered by Peruvian legislation regarding marketing abroad in this period were as follows:

- The Customs Code of 1920 banned the import of drugs or pharmaceuticals into Peru if their contents were not clearly printed on their containers.
- Act 4428 of 26 November 1921, which was to become normative in the entire period, concentrated the drug trade in Callao for better state control and required prior authorization before any foreign trade operations could be carried out.
- Through the Supreme Resolution of 16 November 1923, the state reserved itself exclusive rights on foreign trade in all substances regarded as drugs covered by Act 4428.

- On 8 January 1926, it was established that the possession of drugs for consumption or sale (under Act 4428) by unauthorized individuals was considered a smuggling offense and the drugs subject to confiscation.

As for domestic drug circulation, Act 4428 established a system that recorded the circulation of drugs covering the activities of manufacturers as well as pushers. The sale of drugs was limited to pharmacies, and the drugs were only available on medical prescription. Prescriptions were only issued by veterinarians or medical practitioners. Official legislation on prescriptions for the use of narcotics was not officially formalized until 1945.

The prohibition of opium dens was also covered under Act 4428. On 30 March 1936, a new Supreme Resolution was passed ratifying all the previous stipulations.

The second stage of Peruvian drug legislation showed that the state was aware of the growing presence of underground drug operations and that their reaction was to stamp down hard. The whereases and herebys of the Supreme Decree of 26 March 1949, showed that the illegal narcotics trade had reached alarming proportions and that it was necessary to repress the activity. Provisions were made to deal with drug trafficking domestically and internationally, which shows that the links between international criminal organizations had been detected. Drug trafficking was no longer just a problem of the Public Health Ministry, it had become essentially a police matter.

In contrast to the first stage of legislation, attention became focused on the manufacture and marketing of cocaine. On 28 March 1949, Decree Law 11005 was issued with its various amendments, and it continued to be the basic legislation in the war on drugs until 1978 when it was completely replaced. Decree Law 11005 was the first serious and detailed effort to categorize crimes related to the illicit drug trade. Activities classified as being of a criminal nature included the manufacture or marketing or any additional action associated with narcotics.

The repressive tone of Decree Law 11005 was pronounced, because it introduced a legal process with few guarantees for the individual and established a court to deal with all trafficking crimes that consisted principally of state administrative officials. These norms continued until 25 July 1963, when the Organic Act of the Judicial Branch (Act 14605) eliminated the special jurisdiction and reestablished the power of members of the judiciary to pass sentence.

Another important feature of the time was the concern—echoed on the international scene—about coca-leaf cultivation in Peru. Degree Law 11046 established the Estanco de la Coca (State Coca Leaf Monopoly) regulating the planting, cultivation, and harvesting of coca as well as its distribution, consumption, and export. Industrialization for medical use was to be regulated by the Health Ministry.

The next important ruling during this period was Supreme Decree 254 of 11 December 1964, which sought to reduce coca cultivation progressively by 10 percent every two years. In other words, coca would cease to be cultivated in Peru within twenty years. The same Supreme Decree also banned the supply of coca to workers as part of their wages or simply as a matter of course during their work.

The third stage of drug legislation began with Decree Law 17505 of 18 March 1969 and continues today. The law focused, legally speaking, on the illicit drug trade as part of a worldwide social problem. The policy of repression was not abandoned but became secondary, at least in theory, with social preoccupation becoming dominant.

The Public Sanitation Code stated that drug addiction was a public health problem, not only because of the harm caused to the addict but because the imitation caused by peer pressure was in danger of giving rise to a problem of endemic proportions. Act 19505, modifying the repressive measures concerning drug trafficking, was passed after the Public Sanitary Code. The act stipulated that it was necessary to differentiate between profit, which was the real culprit, and use. Repression was redirected toward this end, and separate measures for control of consumption and protection, particularly in cases involving minors, were designed.

Next, Decree Law 22095 of 21 February 1978 was issued, consolidating all of these new trends and establishing their main aims:

- repressive measures directed at the trafficking of addictive drugs;
- prevention of unlawful use;
- drug addict physiological, psychological, and social rehabilitation programs; and
- reduction of coca-leaf cultivation.

Decree Law 22095 fully recognized the existence of a highly organized international trade in illicit drugs. It made it a crime to promote, organize, finance, or lead rings or groups of individuals involved in domestic and international drug trafficking.

It is significant that all this legislation falls within what was agreed at the International Conference on the Improper Use and Illicit Trafficking in Drugs, Vienna, June 1987. Peru was approaching the drug-trafficking problem more from the outside than from within. This approach shows that both producer and consumer nations are united in the ideal of stamping out drug trafficking, even if their separate approaches and problems are different.

Finally, from 1982 to 1985 five laws were established that at best revealed a clumsy handling of matters that might easily have initiated harsher persecution of the drug rings, but instead ensured that more run-of-the-mill crime received greater leniency compared to serious offenses. It was naturally assumed that those convicted of drug offenses should be deprived of privileges, such as parole, probation, and so on; however, at the same time, some held with the theory of being as lenient as possible with the defendant and also supported the precept of criminal law (as recognized by Peru's Constitution) that the law should be applied with hindsight, taking good behavior into account (Article 187 of the constitution). Thus, what happened was that every time there was an exception in the application of this leniency in the cases of drug traffickers, it was to the advantage of all those who had been condemned up to that time as well as of those whose cases were currently being heard. This way, except for pardons (which continued to be prohibited in the five norms), all the other benefits could be used by the traffickers.

CONSIDERATIONS FOR THE FUTURE

While Peru was evolving its legislation, it was nevertheless obvious that the government had no definite stance on drug trafficking. If Peru had been serious about eliminating the drug trade then it ought to have developed solutions that dealt more specifically with its own situation and not merely emulated other countries. These are the facts: after seventy years of pursuing a policy of repression, extensive coca-leaf production has developed and prevailed. The imported solutions have not worked and clearly demonstrate that an approach based on imitation rather than on a native, tailor-made design—despite any shortcomings—is doomed to repeated failure. Peru should completely rethink its coca-leaf strategy and come up with its own alternatives in order to deal with drug trafficking. In this way, it would be contributing to the solution of the problem on an international level.

Drawing up the general strategy for redevelopment is not part of current legislation, but it does reflect it, and it would be well worth investigating which law might contribute to its design and successful application. The redevelopment strategy is a central issue because if it is assumed that the drug trafficking problem were to be easily solved, certain areas of the population who make their living in whole or in part from drug trafficking would find themselves against the wall both financially and socially. Considering the extent of drug trafficking in Peru, this is a point that is too important to be ignored.

It is clear that neither regionalization nor agriculture and livestock development policies have taken the effects of drug trafficking into account. Both areas should therefore be investigated, and each area of legislation studied.

It is noteworthy that although the laws on drug trafficking include the analysis, on the whole they look like afterthoughts to existing measures, failing to take into account the peculiarities pertaining to Peruvian drug trafficking. This urgent need for a more systematic approach just goes to show that the drug problem does not afflict the Ministry of the Interior but the entire government apparatus.

The roles to be played by regional and local governments in the war on drug trafficking is also worth studying. Currently, it would appear that the drug trade is not considered to be their problem. Lastly, how should the state financial policy as well as those of the public and private financial institutions combat the illicit drug trade? None of these last points has ever been properly analyzed or written into the law in Peru.

One of the most efficient ways of fighting drug traffic rings is through the income tax system, paying particular attention to external signs of wealth and similar indicators. The Peruvian tax system includes such measures but they have been disregarded. A closer look at its possibilities would be useful, indeed to an efficient campaign.

Jurisdiction is a key problem that embraces two aspects: the security of magistrates, and the effectiveness of the legal process. First, court magistrates must be protected from violence so that their decisions can remain impartial. Unfortunately, they are not adequately protected and are constantly under threat and wide open to attack. In Peru, when a judge is assigned to a court or tribunal handling drug trafficking or terrorism cases, it often means that he is being reprimanded or that it is a political maneuver by one of the superior courts or even the supreme court itself. Urgent reforms are needed in this area of the crisis.

Second, the security measures currently in effect were designed to protect individuals or small groups of offenders but have no capacity to stand up to the international criminal organizations whose arsenal of resources allows them to exploit every legal loophole in a drug trafficker's defense. It is vital then to reorganize the legal system in such a way that would exclude the exploitation of the law but that would not affect the rights of the individual. It will not be easy, but a balanced solution needs to be found fast.

Lastly, it is interesting that corruption has not been considered a central issue in forming legislation. This is a particular cause for concern in the drug war, not only because it is capable of undermining the state and the establishment but also because the decision that the individual has to face is one of either accepting the bribe or of becoming a casualty. Drug trafficking leaves very little freedom of choice. Obviously something must be done about this vicious corruption. Judges simply cannot be left in such a dilemma (between the drug traffickers and state repression), and whatever is done should be made law. It is obvious that Peruvian legislation is designed to punish people who are willingly corrupted and is useless when it comes to the complexities of the drug trade regarding this point. Nothing is being done to modify this area of the Peruvian legal system.

Drug trafficking is a medical, social, and criminal problem and contains many areas where legal reform would be a useful part of a combined campaign against drugs, but it must be done soon.

STRATEGIES FOR THE DRUG TRADE

Combatting the drug trade involves two different approaches, first, designing a suitable strategy and, second, analyzing the problems sufficiently, in order to be able to arrive at the most effective solution. The strategies that apply to Peru as well as to the rest of the world fall into two categories: (1) legalization, or (2) since drugs remain illegal, establishment of the roles that separate nations should play within an overall strategy.

Some experts propose the legalization of the use of drugs. Ethan Nadelmann supports this view with the following arguments:

1. Current drug control measures are defective and will continue to fail.
2. Many of these measures are costly and become counterproductive. Much of the harm identified with the drug problem is actually caused by prohibition policies.
3. There are good reasons to dispel the fear that legalization would lead to mass abuse.[13]

On their own, none of these arguments would achieve the desired results. Let us assume that Nadelmann's first argument is true (and there is evidence to that effect). Where are there any better policies to replace them, and would legalization be any more effective?

Nadelmann's second statement is also true in that, to date, measures have encouraged prices to rise despite oversupply. The U.S. consumer price has not dropped despite price reductions in the stages leading up to marketing but this is not necessarily a recommendation for legalization either.[14] A better idea might be to avoid the same mistakes and to completely redesign existing policy.

Nadelmann's third statement is pure hypothesis, and there is no reason to presume it to be correct. Basically, Nadelmann's arguments are not convincing enough to justify legalization. Other sources back legalization because they maintain that drugs are freely available and profits are so high only because the drug trade is an underground activity. The only way to fight drugs would be in a situation where access and prices were maintained at levels at which dealers would find it impossible to compete.

To put the preceding arguments into practice would require the following:

the producer would buy up the surplus coca and the consumer the finished or semi-finished product at reasonable prices (for the consumer nation, "reasonable" would fall somewhere between the cost of production and the price paid by the trafficker). The nations involved would have exclusive buying rights to the product at every stage of production and would have to tackle the problem at every opportunity, not just in the marketplace. There would be agreement to deal with the most pressing problems first, both in consumer and producer countries, and the accord could be extended. Resulting profits to the producer nations would go toward developing the coca-growing areas. And consumer nations would use the drugs to treat their addicts with a view to discourage their use.

The debate as to whether cocaine is addictive is relevant in this regard. Dr. Ramiro Castro de la Mata, medical authority on the subject, states the following in a special report commissioned for this study:

Some influential groups maintain that cocaine used recreationally by intelligent people is completely safe. . . . But if you inject or smoke it, once you are hooked all the intelligence in the world won't do you any good. . . . There are some very convincing arguments around and the idea would not be so radical if cocaine were not so addictive. However, because of the psychopathic tendencies it produces in addicts, it would be very dangerous to increase its availability. One need look no further than crack, a cheaper and far more addictive form, for an example of this. . . . Cocaine affects everyone in the same way regardless of age, intelligence, class, creed, or financial status.

Legalization might nevertheless prove futile if, for example, the crack problem continues to spread, for two reasons: (1) no government could ever contemplate legalizing a drug like crack; and (2) if crack production could be developed straight from the basic paste without having to be refined into cocaine first, then costs would be substantially reduced, and the drug rings would be in a better position to compete in a legal market.[15]

Current prohibition strategies do not contemplate legalization. The strategies are being developed by the producer nations, by consumer nations, and in joint efforts.

Responsibility of the Producer Nations

As Barsallo and Gordillo conclude:

The consumer nations do not think that the blame for the problem is theirs since production takes place outside their borders and their main efforts are to keep the drugs out. In addition they send "economic aid" to the producer countries to help them eliminate "their drug trafficking problem" via crop eradication.[16]

Strategy also includes dropping penalties for its use (concentrating on production and marketing), crop substitution, threatening or imposing sanctions on nations who do not tow the international line, using troops for crop eradication (like Bolivia in the mid-80s) and reducing the impact of coca production on the underdeveloped producer nations.

As the world's leading consumer, the United States follows this policy religiously. As Diego García Sayán writes:

This being such a sensitive issue in U.S. foreign policy makes it a possible area of confrontation if the Bush administration ever gives its blessing to the use of military force. . . . If it ever became a question of "national security" then U.S. intervention in Peru would be a reenactment of what has happened in some Central American nations.

Obviously if the argument for approaching this problem in a similar style to other "low-intensity conflicts" were to gain ground, resulting in increased CIA and National Security Council intervention, a possible outcome would be the militarization of the war on drugs, perhaps producing some terrible consequences for the Andean countries, as well as a threat to their sovereignty.[17]

The U.S. position on this point is still unclear. On one hand, Bush has recognized that responsibility should be shared. On the other hand, the idea, eventually abandoned, of sending ships to blockade the Colombian coast, and the invasion of Panama, reveal that the United States shows a tendency toward this sort of action.

International strategies have so far failed dismally in the war on drugs. In fact, Nadelmann states somewhat sensationally, although accurately: "International drug control rhetoric focuses on the complete eradication of marijuana, cocaine, and heroin. But the truth of the matter is that it is impossible to eliminate drug trafficking, and that the real aim of the drugs war is to keep drug retail prices as high as possible."[18]

Responsibility of the Consumer Nations

The position of the consumer nations is the antithesis to that of the producers. To further quote García Sayán:

Clearly, the "co-responsibility" theory distorts the truth of the situation. There is a central responsibility among those who are involved in the business. Therein lies the problem. It is, however, easier to "concentrate our efforts in the fields of Peru where 300,000 campesinos grow coca, than it is to jail the pusher on the street corner" (quotation from a speech by Nancy Reagan).[19]

Contrary to popular belief, U.S. drug traffickers do far better from the illicit drug trade than their counterparts in the producer nations. A report by the Special Senate Committee on Causes of Violence and Alternatives for Peaceful Settlement of Disputes in Peru showed that a kilogram of cocaine costs about US$17,000 in Peru and sells for around US$76,000 in the United States.[20]

Nadelmann states:

The price increase in cocaine between the Colombian airfield and the Miami wholesaler is only fivefold from about US$3,600 to US$4,000, to between US$17,000 and US$22,000 per kilo. However . . . the final street value of cocaine . . . is around US$80,000 to US$120,000 per kilo—seven times its original value. Since many Colombians also run the transport and primary distribution networks, the number of times that they manage to increase the price of the product is truly dramatic.[21]

Quoting the *Economist*, Campodónico states: "of the US$20-to-25 billion wholesale value, the Latin Americans get back anything between US$3-to-6 billion of which 50 percent goes to the Colombians with the rest being divided up more or less equally between Peru and Bolivia."[22] And Nadelmann concludes: "The initial price of cocaine is about 20 percent of its original U.S. wholesale price and only about 4 percent of its final retail price, despite the strenuous attempts made in the fight against drugs."[23] Thus, using these figures as a rough guide, we show that the lion's share of the money from drug trafficking goes to the United States not Latin America and, therefore, most of the money laundering as well. Consequently, one could easily assume that if there were no market for a product that sold for US$76,000, five times its original price, then the illegal drug trade would not exist.

Landing responsibility on the consumers is really a way of making them shoulder the financial burden. García Sayán says:

What we need is for the U.S.A. to provide us with a massive amount of resources, in a kind of "Marshall Plan," which would not only provide long-term subsidies for the redevelopment of the coca-growing areas, but also other forms of promotion (giving preferential treatment to Peruvian products in U.S. markets) as well as help with the balance of payments, which would allow other resources to be directed towards the generation of foreign exchange to replace that generated by coca.[24]

Co-responsibility

This strategy implies that the producer and consumer nations should share the problems and benefits of the drug war. Both producer and consumer nations—the United States in particular—should move away from the theory that the producer nations are the cause of the problem. First of all, the roles of each group need to be established. Consumer nations obviously need to prevent the drugs from entering the country and should do what they can to stem production. How should these financial considerations be worked out? With the sums involved, it is obvious that the underdeveloped nations will be financially out of their depth, and the developed nations will have to make a real effort to find the resources.

Do the producer nations, however, have the right to demand compensation as part of the overall solution for the resulting economic and social upheaval? This is an important issue since many people live off drug trafficking. The Special Senate Committee on the Causes of Violence and Alternatives for the Peaceful Settlement of Disputes in Peru estimates "that there are no less than 60,000 families, roughly equivalent to 300,000 Peruvians, growing coca, most of whom are campesinos depending illegally on coca to survive."[25] Barsallo Burga and Gordillo Tordoya also say: "It is estimated that 120,000 families, roughly 600,000 people, are involved or dependent on the illicit production of coca and this figure is growing rapidly."[26] How would these hundreds of thousands of people be affected? With co-responsibility, this problem would be sorted out with the help of a partner.

Producer nation economies have become "drug addicts" due to the fact that drug money has been assimilated into their overall financing. It was estimated that Peru had to monetize US$1,412 million to finance its part in the drug-trade cycle.[27] Should the consumer nations have to agree to compensate for a nation's lost illegal revenue as part of eradicating the drug problem?

In a special report prepared for this study, Dr. Manuel Moreyra, a Peruvian lawyer and economist, says:

In order to have a significant effect on drug trafficking, an economic policy coordinated with foreign aid is urgently needed to compensate for the loss of illegal revenue. Today, Peru is addicted to this flow of foreign currency that has given rise to economic policies that count on this money. Obviously this is very dangerous in the long term. Nevertheless the sudden removal of this source of revenue would have drastic consequences. Compensation for this loss could be achieved by promoting legal exports and protecting local manufacturers principally through the exchange rate. In the meantime, investment from abroad would be required to promote agriculture, agribusiness, infrastructure, training, education, and new commercial opportunities. The money used to service the foreign debt could go toward this end. Other funds could be used to buy up part of the coca crop while the crop substitution was in its transition period. But it is important to remember that isolated efforts are no good and that a carefully planned macroeconomic strategy that will keep human suffering to a minimum is what is really needed. The General System of Non-Reciprocal Vertical Preferences of the United Nations' Conference on Trade and Development (UNCTAD) would guarantee privileged access to the large consumer nation–markets for certain products in order to develop dynamic sectors in the producer nations while economic aid would be directed at the suppression of drugs.

Despite all its problems there is no doubt that co-responsibility is the right approach to an international solution because it takes into account all sides of the problem. These considerations should be reflected in the finished agreement on an international strategy that at the moment reflects the Vienna Convention, which places responsibility with the producer nations.

SOLUTIONS

As far as reaching a solution to the drug problem is concerned, it is important to recognize that the crux of the matter is not the existence of consumers and producers but the traffickers themselves. It is fundamental to draw up a list of measures to be considered, which would cover all the main points.

Tackling Production

Even though it is increasingly apparent that the producer nations assign more and more value to the coca leaf harvested,[28] the producers basically harvest the leaf and/or take it through the first stage of refining, and the consumers are the persons who buy the finished product. The real drug trafficking occurs in between these two points, that is in refining, transport, marketing, and financing.

To tackle this problem requires a coordinated offensive against production and distribution to correct current methods that are haphazard:

1. There are few light plane manufacturers, and yet to date their operations have been tracked sketchily at best.
2. Sale of vital refining chemicals like kerosene, acids, alkalies, and oxidants, are unregistered. Steps might easily be taken to monitor such sales.
3. Effective air traffic control in either consumer or producer nations is nonexistent. For instance, it seems odd that Florida's airspace is violated daily by planes transporting drugs, but that any military plane invading U.S. airspace is immediately detected.
4. Control of sea, river, and overland traffic is also pitifully inadequate. This situation should be remedied.
5. The money-laundering issue has never been seriously confronted.

It is important to maintain suppression of the drug trade. There is still plenty that could be done on this front. Co-responsibility would seem to be the most effective way of dealing with suppression.

Dealing with Corruption

With the amount of money generated by drug trafficking, it is not surprising that corruption results, as has been documented in the report by the Special Senate Committee on the Causes of Violence and Alternatives for the Peaceful Settlement of Disputes in Peru:

Due to the growing power and influence of the drug trade, the establishment has become riddled with corrupt officials and has actually reached the scale of a national crisis in which the public image of state institutions and power groups is tarnished by the pervading atmosphere of mutual distrust between them. The records show that a good many magistrates and High Court judges have been caught and thrown out of office following charges, although none has ever actually been convicted, a fact that the Drug Traffic Investigation Committee [Comisión Investigadora de Narcotráfico] sees as a sort of sanctioning of corruption. Similar cases, including those involving high-ranking officers, have been recorded in the police force. Corruption has reached ministerial level, a situation that must make public officials wonder how bad the situation really is, apart from it being demoralizing for the man in the street.[29]

A glance at the Political Chronicles (Cronología Política), an unpublished work by the Center for Development Studies and Promotion (Centro de Estudios y Promoción del Desarrollo, DESCO) for 1987 and 1988 reveals the apparent involvement of prosecutors; all ranks of police; prison guards; stockholders in newspapers and financial institutions; as well as municipal council and congress members. The term "apparent" is used because as yet no convictions have been handed out. However, the slightest link of important public figures to the world of drug trafficking is in itself a cause for grave concern.[30]

Corruption is certainly not confined to Peru: U.S. institutions have also been implicated in money laundering and drug financing operations.

Despite the fact that the U.S. government demands that its Andean partners use political force to combat drug trafficking, it refuses to confront powerful financial and industrial interests in the United States which are obviously doing well out of the cocaine industry. About 95 percent of chemicals needed in the trade start their lives in the United States, and yet the U.S. government demands the eradication of the coca crop of small-scale farmers by force while it politely asks its own companies to please refrain from supplying their products when links with drug trafficking are suspected. In addition, the increase in dollars coming into the United States as a result of the trade has generally been ignored. Despite the heavy publicity given to the crackdown on money laundering, the U.S. government still tolerates its virtual institutionalization in Florida's banks.[31]

The following need to be reviewed in both producer and consumer countries:

- The effectiveness and honesty of the judicial system;
- The effectiveness and honesty of the police and military;
- The quality of the legislation used for the suppression of drug trafficking, for dealing with corrupt public officials (who often receive less harsh sentences) and for investigating private fortunes for tax purposes;
- Jurisdictional procedures, which are out of date, no good for witness and court official security and that are also inadequate on the subject of the theory of proof;
- State institutions that fight drug trafficking because prisons, police, the judiciary, and so on would all benefit from a greater degree of coordination; and
- Adequate pay for officials involved in drug trafficking control.

Here again the degree of collaboration afforded by the co-responsibility strategy leads more than any other to a successful solution to the problem.

Public Opinion

Public opinion in both Peru and the United States must be awakened to tackle drug trafficking successfully so that the measures employed can receive full support. However, statistics suggest that the U.S. public is not universal in its condemnation of drug trafficking. The National Drug Abuse Institute as quoted by Barsallo and Gordillo, indicate that forty-seven million people in the United States take drugs, that is, one in four.[32]

Peruvians, on the other hand, condemn use more than production: "Public opinion can be divided into two categories. The first, supported by the media, maintains that cocaine basic paste is a trafficking problem. The second, the man in the street, says that cocaine basic paste is a consumer problem."[33] Such diverse opinions are not conducive to eliminating consumption in the United States or production in Peru. Here again, the co-responsibility approach is the best.

Crop Substitution

An important aspect to bear in mind is the difference between the campesinos and the single-crop coca producers in the coca-growing areas like Huallaga. Carlos Aramburú states:

We should take care in evaluating who should benefit from development. The single-crop producer is usually an outsider with no roots in the area who is financed by drug traffickers who deal in basic cocaine paste. He must not be confused with the settler farming a range of crops whose life is dedicated to agriculture and who has lived in the area for years.

When repression affects both of the above then our efforts are misguided. Bona fide farmers and cattlemen settling in the high jungle need our support, which includes security of land tenure, attractive price deals, and technological aid to promote crop substitution. Much larger donations than have so far been received are needed to achieve this as well as relaxing property ownership laws.[34]

The following recommendations should be borne in mind: (1) a plan to administer credit to farmers in coca-growing areas in order to promote the production of legal crops is vital to the fight against drug trafficking; and (2) crop substitution should also reflect this strategy and be for real farmers.

Crop substitution involves prices and markets. Barsallo and Gordillo note:

The high profitability of coca has led to a drop in staple crop production and caused heavy migration toward the coca-growing areas. Each hectare produces a metric ton of coca leaves, estimated at US$5,300. Since on average a farmer owns three hectares, he will have an approximate income of US$15,900, while other crops over the same area will yield the following income: bananas, $3.23; corn, $2.71; rice, $3.23; cacao, $9.69; coffee, $2.71; *annatto* (an extract of the bixine plant, used as dye), $1.085.[35]

Aramburú goes on to add:

In our 1985 survey, we found that from 1980 to 1985, the production costs of four of our most important tropical crops (rice, corn, yucca, and banana) rose by between 350 percent and 529 percent, that is, four to six times more than their prices, which increased by 60 percent to 120 percent. There was also a parallel drop in the productivity of coffee, corn, banana, and tea as well as a stagnation in rice and yucca yields. Coca production, meanwhile, grew 60 percent over the same period, its price reaching US$115 per *arroba*, a gross annual income per hectare of US$18,400 to US$20,000.[36]

In this situation, crop substitution is unlikely to succeed. Farmers would probably accept less income from a legal crop, but they are unlikely to do so faced with these figures.

Quoting the Andean Report (an English language economic monthly magazine published in Peru) on crop eradication, García Sayán points out that the rate of elimination of the coca shrubs during the first three years of the program was as follows: 1983, 2,651.93 Ha (1.7 percent of the total); 1984, 3,840 Ha (2.5 percent of the total); and in 1985, 3,773 Ha (2.5 percent of the total). In addition, these figures are totally insignificant since new cultivation has outstripped the eradicated areas.[37]

Barsallo and Gordillo explain the situation in the following way: "The mature plant requires four to five workers to loosen the soil with picks before pulling it up, making the operation extremely slow."[38] As these authors later add,[39] the only surefire way to carry out eradication effectively is to use herbicides, which is ecologically questionable. Crop eradication would, therefore, not be a realistic short-term solution.

CONCLUSIONS

The best approach to solving the drug problem is, unquestionably, co-responsibility even though it would be extremely difficult to evaluate the separate roles of the nations. The solutions to be urgently implemented in a coordinated fashion are as follows:

1. The main thrust of the campaign should focus on drug trafficking itself, as opposed to consumption or coca production. Indispensable measures not yet taken include tackling the media, establishing controls over access to inputs, and instituting effective sanctions for money laundering.

2. Producer nations and consumer nations should address corruption—which is preventing a solution to the drug problem. Nations will have to guarantee the honesty and effectiveness of their law-enforcement agencies, as well as the quality of their repressive legislation. In addition, they will need to guarantee the security of judges and pay their law-enforcement personnel adequately.

3. A public awareness drive is urgently needed to discredit both consumption in the consumer nations and production in the producer nations.

4. Crop substitution may be part of a solution in the long term, but it is subject to a number of conditions: (a) the distinction between traditional farmers who grow coca on the side and single-crop producers who grow nothing but coca and rely entirely on the mafias; (b) credit and other additional measures to safeguard alternative production; and (c) the guarantee of profits for alternative produce in the medium term.

5. Coca-leaf eradication does not appear to be a realistic solution. If carried out manually, paltry progress is made, and if herbicides are used, ecological disaster could result.

NOTES

1. In economic terms we calculated that Peru's total cocaine output in 1989 reached 270,000 tons.

2. J. M. Jutkowitz, R. Arellano, R. Castro de la Mata, P. B. Davis, J. Elinson, F. R. Jeri, M. Shaycopt, and J. Timaná, "Uso y Abuso de Drogas en el Perú," Monografía de Investigación No. 1, Lima, Perú: CEDRO, 1987, pp. 92–95.

3. Roberto Lerner, "El impacto de las drogas en el Perú. El caso de la cocaína," Unpublished essay, Lima, CEDRO, 1988.

4. Ibid.

5. This estimate corresponds to 1989. Previously, in dealing with chemicals and materials as inputs, the estimate was taken as 200,000 metric tons.

6. Lerner, "El impacto de las drogas en el Perú." Source: Apoyo S.A.

7. Moisés Bayona, *Valor de la inversión en coca* (The Value of Investing in Coca). Lima, Instituto de la Coca; Adolfo Figueroa and Farid Matuck, "Estudio sobre la fuerza laboral y mercado de mano de obra en el Alto Huallaga," Unpublished document.

8. Source: Periodic surveys by the Palma del Espino Company.

9. C. E. Aramburú and E. Bedoya, "Poblamiento y Uso de los Recursos en la Selva Alta: El Caso del Alto Huallaga" (Population and Use of Resources in the Upper Jungle: The Case of the Upper Huallaga) in C. E. Aramburú and C. Mora (eds.), "Desarrollo Amazónico: Una Perspectiva Latinoamericana" (Amazonian Development: A Latin American Perspective), Lima: CIPA-INANDEP, 1986, pp. 115–77.

10. Marcelo Buenaventura, "Victims of Drug Trafficking," *Medio Ambiente* (Environmental and development magazine) No. 23, September 1987, pp. 8–10.

11. José Barsallo Burga and Eduardo Gordillo Tordoya, *Drogas, responsabilidad compartida* (Drugs, Shared Responsibility). Lima: J.C. Editores S.A., 1989.

12. Lerner, "El impacto."

13. Ethan Nadelmann, "Víctimas involuntarias: Consecuencias de las políticas de prohibición de drogas" (Unwilling Victims: Consequences of the Drugs Prohibition Policies), *Debate Agrario*, no. 7 (Lima: CEPES, July–December 1989), 128–29.

14. Ibid., 139–40. See also Diego García Sayán, "Narcotráfico: El emperador está desnudo" (Drug Trafficking: The Emperor Has No Clothes), *Debate Agrario*, no. 6 (Lima: CEPES, April–June 1989), 56.

15. José Barsallo Burga and Eduardo Gordillo Tordoya, *Drogas, responsabilidad compartida*, 64. Also see Diego García Sayán, "Narcotráfico," 68.

16. Barsallo Burga and Gordillo Tordoya, *Drogas, responsabilidad compartida*, 70.

17. García Sayán, "Narcotráfico," 58–65.

18. Nadelmann, "Víctimas involuntarias," 39.

19. García Sayán, "Narcotráfico," 56.

20. Comisión Especial del Senado sobre las Causas de la Violencia y Alternativas de Pacificación en el Perú (Special Senate Committee for the Causes of Violence and Peaceful Solutions in Peru), *Violencia y pacificación* (Lima: Centre for Development Studies and Promotion (DESCO) and Comisión Andina de Juristas, 1989), 268.

21. Nadelmann, "Víctimas involuntarias," 139.

22. Humberto Campodónico, "La política del avestruz" (The Ostrich Policy), in Diego García Sayán, ed., *Coca, cocaína y narcotráfico. Laberinto en los Andes* (Coca, Cocaine and Drug Trafficking. Labyrinth in the Andes) (Lima: Andean Legal Commission, 1989), 392.

23. Nadelmann, "Víctimas involuntarias," 139–40.

24. García Sayán, "Narcotráfico," 66.

25. Comisión Especial del Senado, *Violencia y Pacificación*, 263.

26. Barsallo Burga and Gordillo Tordoya, *Drogas, responsabilidad compartida*, 59.

27. Juan Briceño and Javier Martínez, "El ciclo operativo del tráfico ilícito de la coca y sus derivados: Implicancias en la liquidez del sistema financiero" (The Operational Cycle of the Illegal Traffic in Coca and Its By-products: Effects on the Liquidity of the Financial System), in Federíco R. León and Ramiro Castro de la Mata, eds., *Pasta básica de cocaína: Un estudio multidisciplinario*. (Lima: CEDRO, 1989), 270.

28. Barsallo Burga and Gordillo Tordoya, *Drogas, responsabilidad compartida*, 64. See also Briceño and Martínez, "El ciclo operativo del tráfico ilícito de la coca y sus derivados," 169.

29. Comisión Especial del Senado, *Violencia y Pacificación*, 263–67.

30. Coletta Youngers and John Walsh, "La 'guerra' contra las drogas en los Andes: Una política mal encaminada" (The "War" Against Drugs in the Andes: A Misguided Policy), in García Sayán, ed., *Coca, cocaína y narcotráfico*, 348–49.

31. "Dossier on Drug Trafficking 1987, 1988." (Unpublished document) Lima: DESCO, 1989.

32. Barsallo Burga and Gordillo Tordoya, *Drogas, responsabilidad compartida*, 52.

33. Delicia Ferrando, "Conciencia social del problema de la pasta en el Perú" (Social Awareness of the Cocaine Basic Paste Problem in Peru), in León and Castro de la Mata, eds., *Pasta básica de cocaína*, 401.

34. C. E. Aramburú, "The Family Plot Economy and Coca Growing: The Case of the Upper Huallaga," in F. León and R. Castro de la Mata, eds., *Pasta básica de cocaína*, 231–59.

35. Barsallo Burga and Gordillo Tordoya, *Drogas, responsabilidad compartida*, 63.

36. Aramburú, "The Family Plot Economy and Coca Growing," 256.

37. García Sayán, "Narcotráfico," 61.

38. Barsallo Burga and Gordillo Tordoya, *Drogas, responsabilidad compartida*, 150.

39. Ibid., 156–57.

BIBLIOGRAPHY

Agencia para el Desarrollo Internacional (United States Agency for International Development). *Coca Corp. Production and Reduction in Peru*. Lima: USAID, 1979.

Aramburú, Carlos E. "La economía parcelaria y el cultivo de la coca: El caso del Alto Huallaga." In Federico R. León and Ramiro Castro de la Mata, eds., *Pasta básica de cocaína: Un estudio multidisciplinario*. Lima: CEDRO, 1989.

Barsallo Burga, José, and Eduardo Gordillo Tordoya. *Drogas, Responsabilidad compartida*. Lima: J.C. Editores S.A., 1989.

Briceño, Juan, and Javier Martinez. "El ciclo operativo del tráfico ilícito de coca y sus derivados: Implicancias en la liquidez del sistema financiero." In *Pasta básica de cocaína*. Lima: CEDRO, 1989.

Cabieses, Fernando. *Etnología, Fisiología y farmacología de la coca y la cocaína*. Lima: Museo Peruano de Ciencias de la Salud, 1985.

Campodónico, Humberto. "La política del avestruz." In Diego García Sayán, ed., *Coca, cocaína y narcotráfico. Laberinto en los Andes*. Lima: Andean Legal Commission, 1989.

Comisión Especial del Senado sobre las Causas de la Violencia y las Alternativas de Pacificación en el Perú. *Violencia y pacificación*. Lima: Center for Studies and Promotion of Development (DESCO) and Andean Legal Commission, 1989.

Dourojeanni, Marc J. "Impactos ambientales del cultivo de coca y la producción de cocaína en la Amazonía peruana" (Environmental Effect of Coca Growing and Cocaine Production on the Peruvian Amazon), in León and Castro de la Mata, eds., *Pasta básica de cocaína*. Lima: CEDRO, 1989.

Echegeray, María. "Actitudes hacia los padres de un grupo de farmacodependientes al alcaloide de cocaína de un barrio de la ciudad de Nueva York" (The Attitudes of a Group of Cocaine Addicts from a New York City District toward Their Parents). Bachelor's thesis in Psychology, Lima, Pontificia Universidad Católica del Perú (PUC), 1989.

Ferrando, Delicia. "Consciencia social del problema de la pasta en el Perú." In León and Castro de la Mata, eds., *Pasta básica de cocaína*. Lima: CEDRO, 1989.

García Sayán, Diego. "Narcotráfico: El emperador está desnudo." *Debate Agrario*, no. 6. Lima: CEPES, April–June, 1989.

Gutiérrez Noriega, Carlos. *Estudios sobre la coca y la cocaína en el Perú* (Studies on Coca and Cocaine in Peru). Lima: Ed. de la Dirección Artistica y Extensión Cultural, Ministry of Education, 1947.

Hanna, Joel. "Coca Leaf Use in Southern Peru: Some Biosocial Aspects." *American Anthropologist* (June 1974).

Hinostroza, Lauro. "Breve informe sobre la coca" (Short Report on Coca). Lima: Departamento de Ciencias Sociales de la Pontificia Universidad Católica del Perú (PUC), 1985.

Jerí, F. *Cocaína 1980*. Lima: Pacific Press, 1980.

Jerí, Raúl. "Tendencias actuales en el tratamiento de la farmacodependencia" (Current Trends in the Treatment of Drug Addiction), *Revista de la Sanidad de las Fuerzas Policiales* (Lima) 45, no. 1 (1984).

———. "Los problemas médicos y sociales generados por el abuso de drogas en el Perú" (Medical and Social Problems Generated by Drug Abuse in Peru). *Revista de la Sanidad de las Fuerzas Policiales* (Lima) 46, no. 1 (1985).

Jibaja, Carlos. "Rol sexual masculino, estudio comparativo entre un grupo de sujetos dependientes a la pasta básica de cocaína y un grupo control" (The Male Sexual Role, a Comparative Study between a Group of Cocaine Basic Paste Addicts and a Control Group). Bachelor's thesis in Psychology. Lima: Pontificia Universidad Católica del Perú (PUC), 1987.

Llerena, S., E. Oliver, and G. Capaña. "Comportamiento antisocial en farmacodependientes a la pasta básica de cocaína" (Anti-social Behaviour in Cocaine Basic Paste Addicts). (Unpublished Document) Lima, 1978.

Mejía Mori, Beatriz. "The Law and Drug Trafficking Cases." In León and Castro de la Mata, eds., *Pasta básica de cocaína*. Lima: CEDRO, 1989.

Morales, Edmundo. "Coca and Cocaine Economy and Social Change in the Andes of Peru." In *Economic Development and Cultural Change*. Chicago: University of Chicago, 1986.

Nadelmann, Ethan. "Víctimas involuntarias: Consecuencias de las políticas de prohibición de drogas." *Debate Agrario*, no. 7. Lima: CEPES, July–December, 1989.

Nizama, Martin. *Sociedad, familia y drogas* (Society, Family and Drugs). Trujillo: Marsol Perú Editores, 1985.

Rodriguez, Alicia. "La psicopatía en la dependencia a la pasta básica de cocaína a través del inventario multifásico de la personalidad de Minesota" (Psychopathy in Cocaine Basic Paste Addiction through the Multi-phase Analysis of the Minnesota Personality). Bachelor's thesis in Psychology, Pontificia Universidad Católica del Perú (PUC), Lima, 1989.

Valdizán, Hermilio. "El cocainismo y la raza indígena: Nota preliminar al estudio del cocaísmo en el Perú" (Cocaine and Natives: Preliminary Note on the Study of the Use of Coca in Peru), *La Crónica Médica* 30: 168–275, Lima, 1913.

Villanueva, Elena. "Consumo de pasta básica de cocaína y características socioculturales en 35 pacientes del Servicio de Consulta Externa del Hospital Hermilio Valdizán" (Cocaine Basic Paste Consumption and Socio-cultural Characteristics in 35 Outpatients at the Hermilio Valdizan Hospital). In the Pontificial Catholic University (PUC)-AID Project: Narcóticos y Educación Pública en el Perú (Narcotics and Public Education in Peru), Final Report, vol. 2. Lima, 1984.

Vinelli, Manuel. "Contribución al estudio de la coca" (Contribution to the Study of Coca), Thesis, Science Faculty of the National University of San Marcos (UNMSM). Lima: San Martin Cia., 1918.

World Health Organization. "Reunión del grupo asesor sobre los efectos adversos de la cocaína" (Advisory Group Meeting on the Adverse Effects of Cocaine). Bogotá, 10–14 September, 1984.

Youngers, Coletta, and John Walsh. "La 'guerra' contra las drogas en los Andes: Una política mal encaminada." In García Sayán, ed., *Coca, cocaína y narcotráfico*, 1989.

Zevallos, Roxana. "Estudio de las actitudes de sobreprotección materna: Una comparación entre un grupo de madres farmacodependientes de pasta básica de cocaína y un grupo control" (Study on Maternal Overprotectiveness: A Comparison between a Group of Mothers Addicted to Cocaine Basic Paste and a Control Group). Bachelor's thesis in Psychology, Pontificia Universidad Católica del Perú (PUC), Lima, 1985.

4

Cocaine: Andean Problems and Andean Solutions

After the case studies of the countries, we present problems common to each and possible solutions, while emphasizing some relevant and often forgotten aspects of the cocaine problem.

THE INTERNATIONAL NATURE OF THE PROBLEM

1. Imprecise use of language has led to labels like "producer" countries (three of the Andean nations—Bolivia, Colombia, and Peru) and "consumer" countries (mainly the United States but also, increasingly, Europe). This distinction is false for the following reasons: Drugs are consumed both in the Andean countries and in the United States, and both areas have to face up to the challenge of how to reduce or eliminate that consumption. On the other hand, it is essential to point out that the North American market plays a decisive role in drug trafficking because of its sheer size and because of the outlandish prices it pays, providing drug smugglers with their profits.

The Andean countries produce coca leaf, but the leaf's transformation into illicit consumer products can only take place thanks to raw materials largely imported from the United States and developed countries in general. The fact that such products are not subject to suitable controls in their country of origin is grounds, strictly speaking, for considering such countries co-producers.

Even though it is not strictly part of the production or smuggling process, drug-dollar laundering is an inseparable part of the illicit drug problem. Here the role played by financial institutions in the United States and the rest of the developed world is fundamental. With very few exceptions, such institutions have so far acted with impunity.

These observations suggest that it would be more appropriate to talk simply about Andean countries, the United States, and Europe. This change would help obviate the frequently committed mistake of blaming "producer countries" for the illicit drug trade.

2. States share responsibility in the fight against the drug trade. It is useless to think that unilateral measures will be effective or that the secret to success lies in persecuting some aspects of the problem rather than others.

The world has coined the concept of "shared responsibility." It assumes the existence of goods that form the common patrimony of humankind and, as such, applies also the distinction between producing and consuming countries. In applying this distinction, emphasis should be placed not just on interdependence but on identification in each country of the specific factors favoring the illicit drug trade; the factors must be shown in such a way that there can be an all-out battle against them.

In the case of the United States, its share of responsibility demands at the very least:

- a drastic cutback in the demand for cocaine and other consumer drugs;
- the establishment of efficient controls—which today are nonexistent—on the inputs needed to process the coca leaf;
- registration and operational control of ships and planes used by drug smugglers;
- controls drastically and efficiently restricting opportunities for drug-dollar laundering;
- action to deal effectively with the drug trade–related corruption inside the country;
- a policy of assistance for Andean countries in their struggle against the illicit drug trade; this policy should encompass both supplies for the antidrug operations and compensatory funds to mitigate the immediate effects of a fall in drug-dollar income, and the policy should also include broader measures such as discussion of the prices and markets open to Andean country exports. For this policy, it is reasonable that the United States should seek the collaboration of other countries, without diminishing its own principal responsibility;
- a campaign among its own population to reduce drug consumption and help the public to become aware of the scope of the problems associated with the drug trade (this campaign should help avoid North American government officials or Congressmen being subjected to pressure from the electorate to take steps that sound impressive but in reality have dubious or harmful consequences);

- respect for the sovereignty and independence of Andean countries and a commitment to abstain from unilateral use of the United States's material strength in the struggle against the illicit drug trade.

As for the Andean countries, their quota of shared responsibility implies at least:

- differentiation between legal and illegal coca and an all-out drive to eliminate illegal coca-growing, its processing, or circulation within each country;
- an integrated and coherent economic policy based on the elimination of illicit drugs, not on its continuing contribution to the economy. The same suggestion applies to national plans for the agricultural sector, which should also contain measures designed to get rid of illegal coca-growing and processing of the coca leaf;
- reduction in the demand for drugs among each country's own population;
- measures in the economic and financial system to prevent money laundering;
- an educational campaign to show the public the multidimensional damage done by the illicit drug trade to the economic and social fabric and thereby to facilitate active participation by ordinary citizens in the struggle against drugs; and
- attempts to increase the level of moral outrage and to combat existing corruption.

3. We consider that the United Nations also has a series of responsibilities, including

- a campaign to make member states more sensitive to the need to inform political elites and the population at large regarding the illicit drug-trade problem, with a view to getting all member states to take part in combating it;
- promotion of an international agreement, similar to the one on piracy, to persecute drug smuggling as a penal offense;
- promotion of international agreements defining and sanctioning white-collar crime, with particular reference to the laundering of drug money and the supply of inputs for processing coca into cocaine; and
- perseverance with efforts to create a new international economic order embodying a more just organization of the world economy, one in which it would be easier to combat the drug trade more efficiently.

4. We consider it correct that we Andean countries should look for our own types of agreement with regard to the illicit drug-trade problem; that we specify our own field of interests within the context of the fight against this

trade; and that we undertake joint action, making use, for instance, of the lobbying procedures that exist in the North American political system.

Our countries should engage in the struggle against drug smuggling because it is harmful to humanity and to ourselves. It is unethical to make this struggle dependent on our obtaining benefits. We do, nevertheless, consider it entirely legitimate to demand that developed countries in general, and the United States of America in particular, should contribute significantly to the costs of the struggle and should establish emergency aid to prevent a crisis sparked by any sudden elimination of drug money.

5. For the struggle against the illicit drug trade to be successful on a truly worldwide scale, reduction in demand and reduction in supply must go hand in hand. If there were to be merely a reduction in the supply of coca from the Andean region, it would then be planted in other parts of the world with a suitable climate, with drug smugglers continuing to earn the profits that today's market provides.

6. The drug trade business is international. It is not just restricted to the production and consumption poles. In our view, in between production and consumption, the following areas have to be tackled:

- control over arms dealing—thanks to the arms trade, drug smugglers enjoy enormous operative and defensive (if not also offensive) capability;
- registration and operational monitoring of seagoing vessels and aircraft that allow drugs to be transported easily;
- production and marketing of inputs needed to process coca leaf, both in Andean countries and in the United States and the rest of the developed world (no real effort has been made to control the circulation of such products); and
- money laundering, mainly through the banks of developed countries.

7. Proper handling of the illicit drug trade problem necessarily involves respecting the sovereignty of states, abstaining from the use of force by one state over the territory or people of another state, and the discarding of such options as threats or pressure to set up blockades or enforce controls in international zones, and so forth. This is not just a question of principle. It is also an operational safeguard because the United States has so far proved incapable of preventing the entry of drugs or of money laundering in its own territory, so that there is nothing to suggest that it would be any more successful outside its own frontiers. It could well, however, do serious damage to its relations with Andean countries.

8. For the struggle against the illicit drug trade to be efficient, bilateral—and even multilateral—relations between the Andean countries and the United States must continue to exist in their own right, regardless of the drug trade problem. Otherwise, recrimination tends to get generalized. There have already been times when relations with the United States were colored by this issue alone: the guarantees demanded by U.S. legislation are a case in point.

9. Trust between states is another prerequisite for the struggle against the illicit drug trade, because it enhances collaboration. An objective glance at relations today suggests that there has so far been more mistrust and guardedness than collaboration. For this attitude to change, new conditions have to be created.

THE UNITED STATES AND THE PRODUCTION, TRAFFICKING, AND CONSUMPTION OF COCAINE

10. The overall political strategy of the United States appears to be based on the quest for economic benefits and the consensus of a majority of its people. U.S. decisions that may strike the domestic population as impressive but do serious damage to Andean countries are both unacceptable on principle and counterproductive as far as the struggle against the illicit drug trade is concerned. The most obvious example of this is that in spite of ten years fighting for the eradication of coca, the cocaine trade has grown enormously and, with it, corruption, violence, and (in countries such as Peru) terrorist subversion.

We consider that U.S. policy is basically repressive in its conception and that this approach is ineffective and even counterproductive. This was certainly the case in the past, but even the apparently less aggressive Bush Plan turns out to have a markedly repressive thrust when one analyzes the content of those aspects of it that have so far been applied in practice.

A key factor worth noting in this context is that, whatever people say, U.S. citizens are consistent about rejecting the production of drugs abroad but not about their consumption. North American statistics themselves indicate that some forty-seven million people have consumed drugs, or roughly one in four of the population. A huge educational campaign is quite clearly indispensable in the United States if this problem is to be tackled.

On the other hand, developed countries that do not have a serious drug-consumption problem generally adopt a passive stance toward cocaine. The measures adopted in the United States have failed, while drug-dollar laundering has been tolerated, all of which naturally benefits the drug smugglers.

11. A gigantic educational campaign is required to get the populations of each developed country backing international policy decisions more whole-heartedly.

12. There is not just a consumption problem in the United States. There is a simultaneous corruption problem that is undoubtedly both sizeable and subtle. Nadelmann and others are surely right when they point out that, well-intentioned or not, the whole anti-drug policy of the United States has so far in practice led to higher prices for drug consumers and hence to significantly higher profits for drug smugglers, especially those based in the United States.

13. It is absolutely essential that the United States confirm that it has achieved a drop in demand proportional to any cutback in supply. It should prove equally that it is preventing a substantial and growing amount of drug-dollar laundering. The well-publicized "impressive blows" dealt so far are not enough.

14. There are signs suggesting that the North American military apparatus might intervene more actively in the struggle against the illicit cocaine trade. These signs include treatment of the illicit drug trade as a national security problem of the United States; military involvement in combatting the drug trade within the United States, a step that for a long time was met with resistance; and the justification of the invasion of Panama on the grounds that General Noriega was linked with the drug trade.

It is important to prevent the militarization of the illicit drug trade problem in the United States because such a strategy is very unlikely to be any more effective than it has been so far.

THE ANDEAN COUNTRIES AND THE PRODUCTION, TRAFFICKING, AND CONSUMPTION OF COCAINE

15. Existing Andean country programs to combat drug trafficking are insufficient. Common approaches must be developed on the basis of rigorous evaluation of each country's particular circumstances and those it shares with others.

Empirical observation in the Andean countries, as well as surveys carried out in Peru, reveal that the population condemns drug consumption and trafficking, but not necessarily production or its effects. This is tantamount to condemning the international drug trade but tolerating the preponderant role that each Andean country plays in the process. This is exactly the inverse of the attitude adopted by the United States, but, in both North America and Latin America, the ones who benefit are the drug dealers.

16. A real educational effort to engage civil society in a more active struggle against drugs is urgently needed. Part of this education involves explaining the evils that the drug trade gives rise to and debunking the idea that it can be economically beneficial.

17. In certain circles in Andean countries, people sometimes justify or pretend to justify various national evils as consequences of the drug trade. Poverty, corruption, crime, and so on may indeed be exacerbated by the illicit drug trade, but they cannot be explained by it alone. Long before the drug problem, Andean countries already suffered from problems derived from their historical formation and social structures. Such problems should be seen in their own right, as well as in relation to the illicit drug trade.

18. People are aware that the production and consumption of drugs are harmful, but people often pay little attention to the various forms of violence drugs foster: corruption of the state bureaucracy, the political elite, armed forces, and police; higher crime rates; alliances between drug traffickers and terrorists; distortion of the class structure; depressive effect on major economic variables, and so on. Here, too, what is needed is a vigorous campaign to educate the public and galvanize societies in the struggle against the illicit drug trade.

ECONOMIC DIMENSIONS OF THE ILLICIT DRUG TRADE FOR ANDEAN COUNTRIES

19. The general public in coca-leaf-producing countries, and even some of these countries' national leaders, often assume that the drug trade is economically beneficial because of the influx of dollars associated with it. Naturally enough, the same people also conclude that if the illicit drug trade were eliminated, their economies would collapse. In this regard, careful distinctions have to be made.

In the very short term, it is undeniable that a drastic elimination of the illicit drug trade would cause serious problems in the economies of coca-leaf-producing countries, including (a) a major drop in disposable foreign currency, causing balance of payments and investment-flow problems in some of the countries; (b) an increase in inflationary pressures due to a rise in the price of imported products; and (c) emigration and social and economic crises in the coca-growing regions, as well as grave social unrest that could spread to other parts of the countries.

Two things must be said about these problems: first, the elimination of the illicit drug trade will not be sudden but gradual, and it will require enormous effort; and second, the coca-leaf-producing countries are going to need emergency aid, if the struggle against the illicit drug trade is to be efficient and rapid.

Above all, the harm that the drug trade does to the economies of Andean countries should not be underestimated. The drug trade yields a proportionately huge amount of low-cost dollars for Andean countries, which depresses the exchange rate, which, in turn, has two effects: exports are discouraged, and the domestic market's level of protection is reduced. Whatever local output is competitive, internationally speaking, becomes less so, especially the agricultural and livestock sector.

Thus, drug dollars begin to substitute for the influx of legal foreign exchange, but also, above all, to undermine a country's capacity to generate foreign exchange. Drug dollars also discourage the setting up of foreign exchange–earning enterprises.

With cheap dollars at their disposal, the authorities may be tempted to lower some prices artificially, creating a kind of consumption illusion and thereby exacerbating the problems to which we have already referred. In the medium term, this weakens the domestic economy and its powers of recovery, fostering new forms of poverty that then interact with various manifestations of violence.

Conversely, it is to be supposed that the elimination of drug dollars, combined, of course, with correct economic policies, leads after an adjustment period to a significant increase in export revenue, to the creation of an economic infrastructure that is more stable and resistant than that of coca, and to improved conditions for farmers. Consequently, it is reasonable to state that the illicit drug trade is economically harmful and destructive for Andean countries.

LEGISLATION AND THE ADMINISTRATION OF JUSTICE

20. A general decline in the ability of the courts to try drug cases is observable in all Andean countries. There are a number of reasons for this, varying from the magistrates' training in penal law to corruption. However, it would be a grave mistake to think that a correct administration of justice is merely a matter of training or moralization. This whole area calls for urgent and efficient corrective action because the attempt to deal with the illicit drug trade through dictatorial methods or brute force, rather than through solid administration of justice, may turn out to be costly in any number of ways.

21. Current legislation regarding the illicit drug trade is mainly repressive and penal: the best laws are those that define the various types of crime most clearly and impose the most drastic sanctions. Recently, the most publicized moves have been extradition and confiscation, which, quite apart from their usefulness and origins, are repressive.

This essentially repressive approach has prevented several rather important aspects from getting the attention they deserve. This includes a major procedural reform designed to ensure that the penal process is efficient in combatting the drug trade. It is worth recalling that current procedures were designed with individual delinquents or small bands of them in mind. Drug smuggling is a global network, with funds at its disposal far greater than those of the vast majority of nations involved. It takes care to remove traces and to use all the legal loopholes it can in its own defense, as well as corruption, threats, and physical violence.

As a result, without sacrificing any individual human rights, we have to look for ways that are viable and compatible with the United Nations Declaration on Human Rights to endow honest judges with both more efficiency and guarantees.

22. There is also the need to redesign political structures and civil society itself, in order to combat the illicit drug trade more efficiently. So long as this struggle is entrusted to the police, the armed forces, and the central government but is not assumed by all state bodies and society as a whole, no victory will be possible.

23. Other ways of persecuting drug smugglers, in addition to penal prosecution, should be established. Tax laws, corrected and properly applied, may be a key instrument. Thus far, they have not been used to the full.

SUBSTITUTION AND ERADICATION

24. We have discussed the problem of crop eradication and found that several years of efforts in this direction have proved completely ineffective: far from diminishing, the number of hectares sown with coca has increased considerably.

Eradication does not prevent a coca farmer moving to another place, deforesting the area, and sowing again. Since this is a mass phenomenon, eradication contributes to ecological damage, however good the intention behind the proposal might be.

Manual eradication of the coca plants requires so much in terms of resources and security safeguards that it is impractical as a priority solution. Eradication by spraying herbicides is an unacceptable ecological risk so long as any doubts remain about it at all, because of the massive amounts that would have to be used to eradicate at least 300,000 hectares dedicated to coca.

25. We consider coca substitution an interesting alternative, as a complement to others, but one of limited effectiveness in the overall context with which we are dealing. Crop substitution may make some sense in the case of farmers who grow coca along with other products. It does not make sense in the case of those whose only link to agriculture consists of deforesting and planting coca.

The substitution required is that of the coca industry as a whole, in other words, the growing and processing of the product. This presupposes the existence of agro-industry and, with it, guarantees for farmers as to their future earnings, which, in turn, implies initial credit, a floor price for output, and access to the appropriate markets.

TRADITIONAL CONSUMPTION AND LEGALIZATION

26. We distinguish clearly between traditional consumption of the coca leaf in a particular Andean culture and the use of its derivatives in the illicit drug trade. We consider prudent the decision to drop the 1961 ban on coca-leaf consumption that was adopted by the United Nations Convention on drugs in 1988.

We have discussed the possibility of legal changes to the current system of penal proscription related to drug smuggling and reached the following conclusions: First, there can be no thought of legalizing the illicit drug trade. We start from an ethical point of view that prevents us envisaging a legalization that, directly or indirectly, might permit the public at large to have free access to drugs. Second, legalizing consumption is a topic considered in connection with opium, a substance that if consumed by a person in certain doses may be compatible with leading a normal life. This is not true of cocaine, a fact that ought to be borne firmly in mind when debating this issue. If consumption were to be legalized, it would have to be as a result of a worldwide agreement and would be harmful outside that context. Legalization ought also to tend toward cutting back consumption, dissociating both consumption and supply from violence, and drastically reducing the market profits enjoyed by drug smugglers today. In short, we do not think that the option of legalization should be discarded a priori. We do, however, suggest that any concrete initiatives in this direction should be preceded by a detailed study of the various aspects involved.

Index

ACDEGAM (Association of Peasants and Farmers of Magdalena Medio), 86, 89. (*See also* Cartels, links with right-wing paramilitary groups
Acullico. *See* Coca, traditional uses
Agroyungas Project (Bolivia), 3
Alcohol misuse, 7
Amazon, 104, 105, 118
Amazon Summit, Brazil, 89–90
American Association of Pharmacology, 50
Andean antidrug strategies, 96–97. *See also* CICAD
Andean Coca Lobby, 37–38
Antidrug trade measures: Bolivia, 16–20, 25–27, 29–39 (*see also* Bolivian Three-Year Plan and Bolivian Five-Year Plan); Colombia, 65–66, 80–81, 87, 90, 94–95; crop substitution and eradication, 14, 17–19, 25, 29–35, 111, 115, 118, 135–36, 149–50; legislation (*see individual countries and international legislation*); Peru, 111, 125–28; repression and military intervention, 21, 23, 27, 30, 44–45, 54, 78–81, 90, 91, 93–94, 123–24, 129, 146 (*see also* U.S. anti-drug strategies);

proposals, 132–37, 141–50 (*see also* Andean antidrug strategies)
Arias Tascon, John Jairo, 95
AWACS (Airborne Warning and Control System), 56. *See also* U.S. antidrug strategies

Barco, Virgilio (ex-President of Colombia), 83, 85, 90, 93–94
Baquero Agudelo, Jesus, 88
Bennett Plan, 36, 39. *See also* U.S. anti-drug strategies
Betancourt, Belisario (ex-President of Colombia), 75, 76
Black market dollars (*see also* Money laundering): Colombia, 58–60, 63–65; Peru, 116–17, 121–22
Blanco, Griselda, 75
Bolivia: agriculture in general, 2–6, 13; antidrug legislation, 2, 16–20 n.23; corruption, 11, 12 n.12, 18, 24; foreign debt, 12 n.12; foreign policy, 23, 25; international image, 23–25; land reforms, 2; macroeconomic impact of coca-cocaine, 8–13; population changes, 3–5, 10, 14 (*see also* Migration); trade unions, 14–15

About the Author

FELIPE E. MAC GREGOR, S.J., editor and president of the Peruvian Peace Research Association, is the author of *Violencia Estructural en El Peru: Marco Teorico* (1990). Other works on the drug problem and violence in the Andes are in progress.